SCOTT WILLS

COMPUTER TIPS for artists, designers, and desktop publishers

W. W. Norton & Company

NEW YORK • LONDON

Other books in the Tips Series:
Complete Studio Tips
Lettering Tips
Tips on Type
Calligraphy Tips
Tips on Making Greeting Cards

A NORTON PROFESSIONAL BOOK

Copyright © 1997 by Scott Wills
All rights reserved
Printed in the United States of America
First Edition

For information about permission to reproduce selections from this book, write to:
Permissions, W.W. Norton & Company, Inc.,
500 Fifth Avenue, New York NY 10110

Designed and illustrated by Scott Wills
Calligraphy examples on pages 44 and 45 by Eliza Schulte
Set in Adobe Alexa and Tekton, and composed in Quark XPress, Adobe Illustrator, and Adobe Photoshop
by Scott Wills
Manufacturing by Courier Westford

Library of Congress Cataloging-in-Publication Data
Wills, Scott.
Computer tips for artists, designers, and desktop publishers / Scott Wills
    p.   cm.
Includes index.
ISBN 0-393-73020-4 (pbk.)
1. Desktop publishing, 2. Pictures—Printing, 3. Desktop publishing industry, I. Title.
Z253.53.W55 1997
686.2 ' 2544536—dc21   97-1077
                                                             CIP

W.W. Norton & Company, Inc.,
500 Fifth Avenue, New York NY 10110

http://www.wwnorton.com

W.W. Norton & Company Ltd.,
10 Coptic Street, London WC1A 1PU

0 9 8 7 6 5 4 3 2 1

This book is affectionately dedicated
to Beth and Gordon Wills

Contents

Preface

This book is loosely structured in sections containing related subjects. It is a sort of patchwork quilt; pick any page at random and you will find a useful piece of information that relates to something elsewhere in the book.

I have written under the basic assumption that the purpose of creating artwork on the computer is to get it out of that computer somehow, whether in print, photo, or electronic delivery form, and to do so with maximum image quality and minimum fuss. A special section deals with prepress and printing issues; another, with electronic delivery issues.

The tips and techniques presented here have worked for me and many of my colleagues. They may not work for all users on all systems. The examples given in this book were produced on a Macintosh system. The predominant applications were QuarkXPress, Adobe Illustrator, Adobe Photoshop, Adobe Streamline, Microsoft Word, and Captivate (for screen captures). Given the similarity in features between popular software programs, most of the techniques that work with these programs on a Mac can be adapted to different programs and platforms, using slightly different tools and commands. Therefore, instead of naming specific applications, I have often used generic descriptors, such as "image-editing program" (instead of "Photoshop" or "Painter"), or "draw program" (instead of "Illustrator," "Freehand," or "CorelDraw").

In many cases, I suggest several alternative approaches to a procedure. I encourage you to try them and experiment to develop your own approach. If you want to expand your capabilities by adding to your tool kit of hardware and software, you will find addresses, phone numbers, or online addresses for resources and suppliers in the back of the book.

If you run across an unfamiliar term, consult the Glossary, which defines terms used in the book, as well as additional common-usage terminology for electronic publishing, design, and printing.

A word about platforms. Although the Mac operating system is the standard for graphic arts production, there is also plenty of work being done on PCs. In the end, unless you have unlimited funds, you must work with the system you have. I have done my best to avoid "platform chauvinism." Most of the tips apply equally to both Mac and PC users; exceptions are noted.

The computer has radically changed many aspects of the ways we work, but one fact remains unchanged: the creative process is a journey of discovery. I wish you a pleasant one.

Acknowledgments

When I began my career as a designer, Bill Gray's first "Tips" books were among my frequent references. Many years later, Bill's work continues to instruct me, and serves as the inspiration for this book. The publishers and I have tried to emulate the format of Bill's hand-lettered books in our choice of calligraphic type and illustration styles.

Thanks to the many colleagues who shared their favorite suggestions, gripes, and workarounds with me, including Gary Brown, Tom Greensfelder, Bob Lightfoot, Francine Ziev, and the STA group. I also thank my Internet pen-pals, whose questions and answers have been part of my education. Thanks to Llana Bernard for her magic keystroking, to Nancy Green for her confidence, moral support, editorial acumen, and steady flow of news from the electronic front, to Selena Leary and Kirsten Miller for excellent proofing and editing, to Liza Schulte for her many questions and for the use of her superb artwork. Gratitude to David Olson, for much good advice, for keeping the machines running, and for helping when they stopped (often at very odd hours). Thanks to Jan DeGoode, Susan Mitz, and Benji Whiteside for pointing the way. Special thanks to Beth and Gordon, to Carol and Catherine, and to Janet for the "writer's retreats." Most of all, thanks to Betsey and Emily for support, understanding, and patience through the long hours of this project, and for reminding me of what's really important.

Getting Down to Business
Steps to mastering your computer and software

1. Read those manuals. Not all are reader-friendly, but they all describe details of the program that you will otherwise miss.

2. Do the tutorials. Even if you don't retain everything you learn, this is a great way to expose yourself to the features and limitations of the application.

3. Register your software. You will be eligible for technical support, notification of upgrades, and special pricing on new versions and related programs.

4. Read. Books, articles, and online information open you up to new aspects of tools you are already using and new tools you could be using. This is a good way to discover the "workarounds" not shown in software manuals. Study printing processes, color theory, typography, composition, and design, too. Learn the principles that will put your tools to effective use.

5. Join a user group. You can find one locally or, if you are located on a remote mountaintop, you can use your modem to contact other practitioners worldwide on the Internet.

6. Take classes, a great way to try out new software and hardware before you buy.

7. Talk to colleagues, especially those who work with your files: service bureau operators, color separators, printers. Establish a network of contacts; you will have expertise at your fingertips, and you won't wear out your welcome with any single resource. Some printers and service bureaus offer training and seminars, too. Form a relationship with a competent computer consultant: the hourly rate you pay will save you countless hours of fruitless trial and error.

8. Experiment. Adapt your work style to your software, and vice versa. Try various methods and several applications to accomplish the same result. Use the ideas in this book as a stepping-off place to develop your own techniques.

9. Learn proper terminology. When your communication is clear and accurate, your work will flow more smoothly.

10. Share what you learn.

Here are some primary sources for locating User Groups. You can find others in seconds on the World Wide Web.

To locate a local Mac user group near you, call Apple's user group hotline, 800 538-9696.

To locate PC user groups, address a letter to:
IBM PC User Group Relations
11400 Burnet Rd., i/z 9623
Austin, TX 78758
or online: IBMpcug@vnet.ibm.com

Setting up a work area

Setting up your office or work space intelligently will pay off many times over. You will work more efficiently, and with more enjoyment. You will be able to find things when you need them. You will look and feel more professional. When starting from scratch, plan to spend at least $5,000 to $10,000 to outfit a single-person office.

Location

If you are setting up a home office, be sure to check zoning regulations before you begin. You may need to clear it with city hall, but don't just ignore the law; getting caught can be costly.

Be sure you have the space you need, and the freedom from distractions you require to do your work. If you plan a home office, designate a dedicated area or room, preferably with its own entrance. Be aware of the requirements for deducting a home office from taxes. Take measurements of the space and furnishings, and draw up a rough floor plan, including work areas, conference area, and storage, taking your working style into account. Strive for flexibility.

Power

If you plan to use electronic equipment, including computers, copiers, coffee makers, etc., try to use dedicated circuits if possible. Put computers, peripherals, and copier on their own circuits; lights, air conditioners, and other items separate. Make sure the wiring is adequate to handle the loads.

Lighting

You need ambient room lighting plus task lights for specific areas. The best light comes from the sun; second-best is full-spectrum artificial light. Full-spectrum fluorescent overheads and halogen task lights approximate the neutral color of daylight, which eases eyestrain and gives a truer hue to reflective colors (such as swatches or prepress proofs). Overheads and task lights should be easily controllable so you can dim or shut them off when viewing your monitor, to ensure accurate color perception.

Monitor calibration is an issue to consider when planning your lighting setup; you need to establish a consistent ambient light for doing color work. Fluorescent lights tend to flicker, which can make your monitor appear to do the same, causing eyestrain.

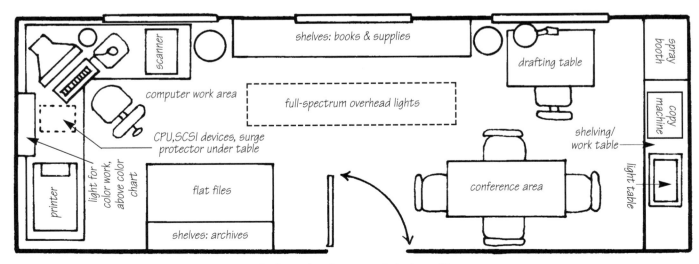

Sample floor plan for a small design office

Phone and fax

It is worthwhile to install two office phone lines: one for voice, the other for fax and modem. An answering device is essential; a useful alternative to the ubiquitous (and short-lived) answering machine is voice mail. It is inexpensive and flexible, and someone else does the maintenance. To eliminate phone interruptions, try this: cut a small square out of cardboard. Write "ring on" on one side, and "ring off" on the other, tape a string to the sign, and hang it by your phone with a push

pin. When you need to concentrate, turn off your phone's ring tone and turn the "ring off" side out. When you are ready to resume receiving calls, switch the ringer and the sign so you can keep track.

Equipment

Buy the best equipment you can afford. A faster computer saves you time and aggravation. One caveat: never buy the first of anything. Wait a few months, let the manufacturer work the bugs out, and watch the price drop from where it was when you first considered purchase. Be careful to choose upgradable equipment, and let it grow instead of just replacing it. A tower-type computer allows the addition of internal disk drives and room for additional RAM. Ports for video and Ethernet capability are desirable.

Discount superstores offer good prices, but may be wanting in the knowledge and service departments; interview salespeople to gauge their expertise and responsiveness. Try shopping for bargains in the back of computer magazines and in mail-order catalogs, where fierce competition drives prices down. You can sometimes find deals on serviceable discontinued or factory-refurbished equipment in the ads. You get the best deals, generally, if you buy "a la carte" instead of getting a package deal. This also allows you to tailor your system and choose better components. Be an informed shopper (see tips on buying equipment in the "Hardware Tips" section).

Along with the electronic devices, outfit your work space with some traditional equipment: a drafting table for drawing and pasteup tasks, a light box or table for tracing and viewing transparencies and proofs, and a color-viewing area with neutral-colored background and lighting. For using spray adhesives and coatings, designate an area with a suitably vented or filtered spray booth (inexpensive cardboard models are available from art supply dealers).

Storage

You can never have too much computer memory or storage media capacity. The importance of backup can't be overstated; you need plenty of drive space for work as well as for backup. A very economical and reliable option is the auxiliary hard drive (internal or external); a gigabyte internal drive is a fraction of the cost of other comparably sized media. Zip and Jaz drives are reliable, economical, and convenient devices. SyQuest drives and cartridges have been the universal standard for file transfer with printers and service bureaus, but they use an outdated technology and can no longer be recommended.

Using a fax/data modem

Invest in a dedicated phone line for your modem; you will work more efficiently and lose less data to interruptions. Be sure, however, to leave "call waiting" off, or program your phone-prefix setting to disable "call waiting" when you fax; otherwise, it will disrupt modem connections.

Although a fax/data modem is indispensable (most modems now offer both capabilities), you may want to have a separate fax machine, too. Faxing by modem can be a convenience, but it can also tie up your computer (which must be turned on), and you can send only computer-generated files (unless you have a Visioneer PaperPort scanner, which functions like an fax input slot for your computer). Some graphics files, such as detailed continuous-tone images or EPS files, travel badly through a fax modem; modem software can only transmit the bitmapped preview portion of EPS files, so that they will printed out as bitmapped versions by the receiving fax. They may come out clearer on the receiving end if you print them out and send by fax machine, especially if halftone mode is available. On the other hand, text and some images captured by fax modem can be printed out with the superior resolution of a laser printer.

If you have several devices on the same line, connect each unit to an automatic telephone line manager (available through electronic stores and catalogs); it reads incoming signals and routes them to the appropriate equipment. You can program your fax modem and machine to determine which picks up a fax transmission first. If you want to save fax messages or run them through an OCR program, set the fax modem to pick up on the first ring.

When you send data by modem, compress large files or folders to save transmission time. A quick and easy way to transmit data is to attach files to an e-mail message.

Get the fastest modem (highest baud rate) you can find at a reasonable price, making sure that it uses a standard transmission rate (33.6 or higher). It should be Hayes-compatible. Modem hardware is the same or similar from brand to brand; the software and support bundled with the modem is what counts. Look for ease of use, versatility, and features (such as auto dialing and broadcasting).

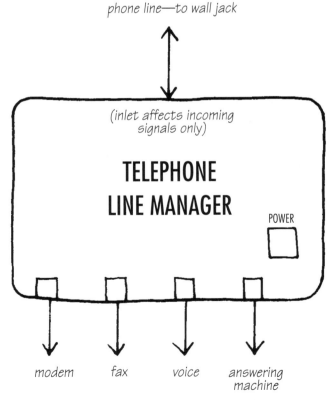

phone line—to wall jack

(inlet affects incoming signals only)

TELEPHONE LINE MANAGER

POWER

modem   fax   voice   answering machine

(outlets individually programmable)

Guidelines for freelancing in electronic publishing

Whether you are just starting out or reevaluating your direction, it is good to have some guiding principles to chart your course through the freelance jungle.

❖ Assess your skills, strengths, and weaknesses honestly: writing, typing, drawing, design, knowledge of processes and media. If you lean toward the technical and have a knowledge base, you may want to try such tasks as stripping and trapping. If you are more of a "right brain" type, leave the technical stuff to the experts, and concentrate on making art.

❖ Determine the types of projects that are currently well within your level of skill and comfort. These will be the profitable jobs.

❖ Avoid the temptation to take on too much. Place a dollar value on your time—the surest way to set limits on your involvement in a project. You can charge a client for producing art, but not for the hours required to learn new software.

❖ Know your customers and define your current and potential customer base. How do they fit with the types of projects you feel you can take on?

❖ Build up a body of successful projects, good samples, and satisfied customers. Although marketing is important, nothing beats word-of-mouth. As your repertoire of skills grows, gradually expand your client base.

❖ Develop a resource network: suppliers, service bureaus, printers, computer users, other freelancers. Be prepared to give help and information as well as receive it.

❖ Keep learning. Invest in courses, seminars, readings, tutorials, support groups, trade shows. Broaden your range. While you are at it, learn something about your customers' businesses, too. They may be paying for your skills, but in the end they are buying your knowledge.

❖ Make transitions as gently as you can. If you have a day job, moonlight until you are fully ready to freelance. Work within your level of skill and equipment capabilities, stretching a little more with each project.

❖ Cover yourself financially, and protect your assets. Establish savings for the inevitable gaps in income associated with freelancing, and use the funds only when you have to. How much to save? Enough to cover six months' living and business expenses is a good place to start. Buy all the insurance you need, including equipment and disability coverage.

❖ Be rigorous in your business practices: don't let record-keeping, billing, payables, and marketing slide. You may enjoy these aspects of your business less than designing or drawing, but they are essential and, in the end, define you as a professional (i.e., one who gets paid for what he or she does well).

How much should you charge?

How much to charge is always one of the most often-asked questions by graphic artists, and the advent of digital tools has not simplified the answer. What you charge depends on a number of factors: your own level of skill and efficiency, your costs of doing business (equipment, rent, etc.), outside purchase costs, and market conditions (the "going rate"; what your customer is willing to pay). To determine price (policy), you need to first determine costs (reality), which will give you your bottom line for profitability.

Establish the bottom line

The average work year totals 1,840 hours. Of these hours, the hours you work fall into two categories: billable (client-directed work) and nonbillable(general business tasks). Your hourly rates need to take both into account. Establish a percentage of unbillable hours (30-50% is reasonable); the remainder are your billable hours for the year.

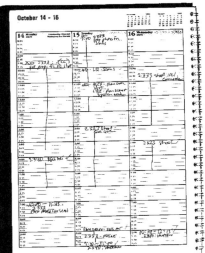

Total your yearly overhead costs (rent, phone, equipment, and supplies) and your living expenses. Don't forget some paid time off for recuperation! These costs should be covered by 1/2 to 3/4 of your billable hours, leaving the rest for profit or reinvestment in the business.

Set a pricing policy

Once you know your bottom line, you can use the knowledge to establish hourly rates or minimum job rates. When bidding on jobs, you may want to base the estimate on the time you think it should take, and add a profit factor (say, 20%), which you may also wish to apply to job costs. You may set varying rates for different tasks or types of projects. Establishing a pricing structure, rather than figuring from scratch each job, will save time, foster consistency, and give you a psychological advantage. The important thing is to base your prices on reality. When quoting a job, spell out clearly what your price includes, and what it doesn't. What you charge for a job should reflect the time you put into it. If unusual circumstances (such as rush work or extensive revisions) occur, factor them in.

Keep good records

In order to charge fairly for your work, you will need a record of how long it took to do, and what you did. Keep a job log. The professional appointment calendars sold at office suppliers work well; you can jot down as you go along what task you are doing and how long it takes. This information is invaluable for estimating future projects, and also supports your billing.

Getting your records and bookkeeping off the page and onto your computer is extremely helpful, but be prepared to invest some money in the right software, and time in finding and customizing it. No single program works for everyone. Some designers customize database programs for their bookkeeping purposes, some use spreadsheets, and some adapt money-management software. A combination of several programs may be the solution, especially if they can interact and exchange data. For a good all-around estimating, time-keeping, job-tracking, billing, and accounting application, Designsoft produces a package of software especially geared to designers and graphic artists.

The other form of records you need are notes and proofs or sketches documenting the progress of the job, and any changes made by you or the client. Keep these at least until the job is finished and paid for.

Undercutting the competition

Competition is a good thing when it encourages quality work and fair pricing. But beware of pricing yourself below your competition (or what you think its prices are) for the sake of getting the job. The graphic arts field is notorious for wildly varying prices for the same type of work because there is no real standard reference for industry pricing in common use by the prospective market. In addition, newcomers constantly enter the field with no clear idea of how to price their services, further clouding the waters. When you arbitrarily lowball a job, you may be pricing yourself below someone who has already lowballed, and didn't have a clue on pricing to begin with. Not a good way to stay in business.

Consult books and articles that deal with pricing and industry practices.

Do your homework, do quality work, save for the slack times, and price for profitability.

Getting paid

Give a careful estimate and establish your terms, in writing. With a new client, get a portion of the total up front and the balance upon delivery. If it appears that the job will run over budget because of client changes or work in addition to original instructions, discuss this as soon as possible; it is hard to negotiate when the job is completed. If you run over budget through your own error, you might try to negotiate a compromise fee; better still, establish a fixed discount in advance. Above all, try to keep the customer happy, and price the next job better. Develop a policy statement so that you are prepared with a response when trouble rears.

Books on graphic arts industry pricing and business practice

Graphic Artists Guild Handbook on Pricing and Ethical Guidelines
Graphic Artists Guild
North Light Books
1507 Dana Avenue
Cincinnati, OH 45207
800-543-4644

Pricing Guide for Desktop Services
Robert Brenner
NADTP Publications
P.O. Box 1020
Sewickly, PA 15143
800-435-7116

The Business Side of Creativity
Cameron S. Foote
W. W. Norton & Company
500 Fifth Avenue
New York, NY 10110
800-233-4830
http://www.wwnorton.com

Working with Your Computer
Organizing electronic files

The proliferation of data files produced by working on the computer makes efficient file naming and archiving necessary. Numerous software packages and individual methods are in use; the key is to find a system that works well for you and those you work with. Here are a few suggestions.

1. Establish and maintain naming conventions for digital files, folders, and storage disks. Name, label, and log all archive disks, storing them so you can easily find and retrieve records. Use general names for folders containing several related file types ("Applications," "Fonts," "Jobs") and more specific names for individual files ("Pagemaker," "Monotype Fonts," "Bob's Menu 1"). Use extensions after the file names to identfy file types (such as ".EPS," ".TIFF," or ".FPO"), especially with graphics files.

2. Do not begin a file name with a space, and avoid using symbols; use only alphanumeric characters. Mac file names may contain up to thirty-one characters, which may include an extension describing the file (such as Swan.Fnl). PC file names are limited to eight characters plus a dot and a three-character extension, indicating the file type (for example, "SWANFNL.EPS").

3. For frequently updated files, you may want to include a sequential number or date in the name. Alternatively, keep subsequent versions of the same art or page layout in the same

file, labeled sequentially. Resave the one you intend to use as "Final" or "Art.fnl." Do not save a revised file with a name identical to that of the original.

4. Print out the menu contents of each storage disk and file the printouts in a loose-leaf binder. In the binder keep a log of all disks out on loan to printers or clients. You can also use software like Iomega's Findit to keep track of files and disk contents.

5. Create a hierarchy of folders (client, job, fonts, art files, layout files). Include a folder containing all final versions of layouts and art, with linked fonts and graphics, which can easily be copied and sent to the service bureau or printer. Copy graphics used in several documents into the "Final" art folder. You can do this easily on a Mac by pressing the option key as you drag the selected file into another folder.

6. Keep a printout of each update to a file. Print the pages or art with a header for identification and date, or note on the hard copy.

Finding lost files

You can help your computer's file-finding command to work more effectively by arranging documents, fonts, applications, and utilities in orderly folders. If you use several drives, or have partitions on one drive, decide which will hold specific types of files.

Frequently used text and graphics (or sounds) can be stored in the Mac's Scrapbook, to quickly copy and paste as needed. More powerful and versatile scrapbook programs, such as Now Utilities' Now Scrapbook, are also available.

Using aliases

To avoid losing new files in the first place, save them to the desktop or to an established "New Documents" folder. Then, at the end of the day, you can easily transfer them to the correct folder.

On a Mac, click the Desktop button when you choose Save. When you quit the application, your new file will be in plain view on the desktop, and not buried somewhere. You now can drag it to the appropriate folder. If you use System 7.5, you can turn on the "Save new documents into the Documents folder" in the control panel; all newly saved files will be placed into the desktop Documents folder.

The Autosave option is a great feature, especially if you have difficulty training yourself to save often. Since Autosave can save updated versions of a file at given intervals, setting the option to overwrite previous versions conserves disk space.

To automatically update files containing changing text or graphics from other files (such as a spreadsheet containing catalog prices), the Mac's Publish and Subscribe feature is useful. Select the data, chart, or graphic, choose Create Publisher from the Edit menu, and the material will be available to another program through an intermediary file. In a word processing or page layout program, use the Subscribe To command to place the chart or data in a document. Whenever information in the original file changes, all linked files will be updated, too.

Aliases help you to locate frequently used files and applications quickly. The Mac's Make Alias command in the File menu creates a copy of the file's name and icon (not the file itself), which can be stored on the desktop or in the Apple menu (a convenient place to access commonly used applications). When the alias is double-clicked, the file or application opens. You can remove the word "alias" from the name; it is not necessary.

To expedite adding new Apple Menu items, make an alias of the Apple Menu Items folder, display it on the desktop, and drop in new items as needed.

You can place aliases of your most-often-used applications into the Startup Items folder; they will open on startup, ready for work.

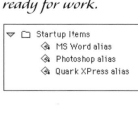

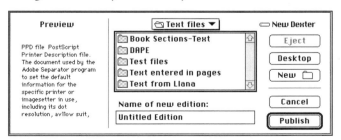

Using template documents

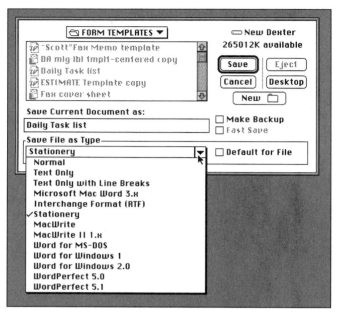

Microsoft Word's Save As dialog box, with Stationery option selected.

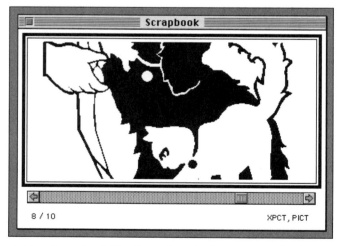

A Mac Scrapbook file. Even though the image is displayed as a portion here, a PICT version of the entire image will appear when pasted into a document.

You can create a template from any Mac or PC document. On the Mac, select the Stationery Pad option in the file's Get Info window, or in the Save As dialog box. After this, whenever you open the document, an untitled copy will be created, which can be saved in a different location by clicking the Save As button. You can use it repeatedly without an accidental change to its contents. This is great for letterheads, form letters, fax cover sheets, logos, and repeating-format documents like newsletters. You can also save often-used text and graphics in the Scrapbook. Scrapbook capabilities can be expanded with alternative software like Now Utilities' Now Scrapbook.

Many applications allow documents to be saved as templates. Keep a folder of frequently used templates, such as business forms, letters, and page layouts.

When you complete a layout or graphic that you want to keep as a model for similar projects, remove the elements exclusive to that job. Save it as a template in your Templates folder. That way, you can retrieve the stationery, business card, three-fold brochure, etc. and simply drop in new copy. Make sure when you do, however, that all specifications for the new job are correct in the template, or update it.

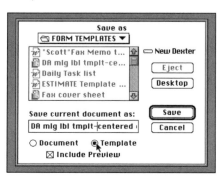

Quark's Save As dialog box, with the Template option selected.

Backup: Avoiding disaster

If the applications you use do not have an automatic Save feature, develop the habit of using the Save command every few minutes—every time you pause in your work.

Next to saving your work often, backing up your computer files is the most important form of preventive maintenance you can perform. Back up to avert catastrophe: whether by fire, flood, lightning, system crash, hard disk failure, or human error, you stand a good chance of losing your files at some time. The remedy requires a full-scale backup system. Back up to recover current work files: Murphy's Law says that your most important document will get erased the day it is due at the printer. Your sole defense is to back up every file on a regular basis.

How often should you back up?

How much work are you willing (or can you afford) to do over? Any backup system should protect you from losing more than a day. Here is a workable plan for a small to medium-sized office.

1. Choose a backup medium (see the list of options at right).

2. Back up at the end of each day, automatically. You can use a utility for this (on the Mac, Norton FastBack, Redux, and Retrospect; on the PC, Cheyenne). Include all data files and documents. Ideally, do incremental backups; that is, sequential copies of documents in progress.

3. At the end of each month, do a full system backup with fresh media.

The optimal backup plan includes at least two copies. This helps to guard against corrupted or outdated files. Almost any backup system is better than none at all!

How you choose to back up depends on: access, convenience, budget, the nature of most files produced, projected level of risk. Consider these, get the equipment and software required, devise a plan, test and refine it, and use it.

Your data will probably fall into these general areas: system files, software, business information (databases, phone lists, financial data), and job-specific files. The first two categories change the least over time, and therefore do not need continual backup; the latter two change daily and so need daily backup. They also grow greatly over time, and so need plenty of storage space. You may want the ability to store particularly sensitive files offsite, safe from fire or theft.

Some backup devices and their capacities

❖ SyQuest drive and disk (44, 88, 105, 200, 270 MB) —Universally accepted for file transfer; expensive and awkward for archiving; technologically obsolete

❖ SyQuest EZ drive and disk (135 MB)—Inexpensive, uncommon

❖ SyJet drive and disk (1.5 GB)—Fast, uncommon

❖ DAT drive—Expensive, but very fast

❖ JAZ drive and disk (1 GB)—A good option for backup, archiving, and transporting large files

❖ Auxiliary hard drive (up to several GB)—Inexpensive and reliable for archiving; difficult to transport

❖ Magneto-Optical drive (128, 650 MB, 1.2 GB)— Common medium for printers and service bureaus

❖ CD-ROM write/record drive (650 MB)—Best suited for permanent files, such as photo images

If you use magnetic storage media such as SyQuest, Zip, or tape drives, move important archive data to new media every five years to guard against deterioration. CDs and optical storage media have more immunity from magnetic drift, and are currently the safest long-term storage.

Since you will also use your storage device to load files for transfer to clients, service bureaus, and printers, poll these groups and find out which media they most commonly accept, then buy accordingly.

Common file types and uses

Most programs allow files to be saved, imported, or exported in several formats. Some programs, such as Photoshop or Hijaak Browser, are useful as "translators," opening a wide variety of image formats, and resaving in the required format. PC format types are generally contained as extensions in the file name. Mac files can be identified by choosing By Kind in the Finder View menu, or by choosing Get Info from the File menu.

ASCII /Text *(American Standard Code for Information Interchange)*. The universal generic text file format, containing only raw text, without format codes or application-specific commands. Can easily be transferred between programs and platforms. Common Windows ASCII extensions for text files: 1st, ASC, ASP, BAK, BAT, CFG, CHP, GEN, INI, ME, OK, OLD, SYD, SYS, TOO. These can be asociated in Windows with NOTEPAD.EXE or another ASCII editor, to expedite file opening.

BMP *(Windows Bitmap)*. Built into Windows and native to Microsoft Paint. Used for PC platform graphics; supports 1- to 24-bit depth and indexed color. Windows extension: .BMP.

CSV. Format for text and data use by spreadsheets.

DCS *(Desktop Color Separation)*. Not a format, this algorithm (featured as a Quark saving option) controls color file output. Files intended for Scitex RIP processing should be saved with this option deactivated.

DIF *(Data Interchange Format)*. Used for saving numbers in individual spreadsheet cells without transferring formulas.

DXF *(Drawing Interchange Format)*. Standard format for 3D and CAD programs.

EPS *(Encapsulated PostScript)*. Image file embedded with PostScript language to instruct a printer or other output device; usually includes a PICT resource file for screen display. May be black-and-white, grayscale, or color, bitmapped or vector-based images. Common uses: saving format of vector-based graphics files (drawing programs), Photoshop duotone bitmapped images, DCS files. Windows extension: .EPS.

GIF *(Graphics Interchange Format)*. Used mainly to save and download online bitmap graphics. Supports 1- to 8-bit colors, limited to 256 colors. Has integrated "lossy" compression. Windows extension: .GIF.

.ico. Windows icon raster format. Can be converted to other graphic formats with Hijaak (on a PC).

IFF *(Interchange File Format)*. Native to the Commodore Amiga, now discontinued. Can be opened in Mac or PC image-editing programs.

JPEG *(Joint Photographic Experts Group)*. Used to save and compress bitmap photo EPS images. A "lossy" compression that allows adjustment in the amount of compression (data discarded), and level of quality (highest quality = least compression). Can reduce the size of color bitmaps up to 95%. Windows extension: .JPG.

LZW *(Lempel-Ziv-Welch)*. Not a format, this "lossless" compression algorithm allows compression of image files without loss of quality.

MacPaint. Bitmap format native to the program.

PCX PC. Paintbrush Extension. Common indexed color PC format, often used for screen captures.

PICS An animation format, essentially a series of PICT images.

PICT/PICT1/PICT2. *Image files, in black-and-white or color, which transfer easily between applications; widely used in Mac platform, especially in video and multimedia applications. Offers "lossless" compression; for 16- or 32-bit images, JPEG compression can be added. If a file is to be output on an imagesetter, it is best to convert to TIFF or EPS; PICT files can cause problems.*

PICT Resource. *Used for startup screens, icons within applications, and screen representations of EPS files. If a file won't open in Photoshop, try opening in this format through the Acquire menu.*

PixelPaint. *Format native to the program. Can be opened in Photoshop.*

PNTG. *Common image-saving format for paint programs. Limited to black-and-white, bitmapped images; limited scalability and print quality.*

RAW. *For exchange of data between applications and platforms; useful when you are not sure which format to use. Saves pixels in binary form (black-and-white).*

RTF *(Rich Text Format). Retains formatted text characteristics for exchange of text between applications. Example: MS Word text saved in RTF for export to Quark document.*

SCITEX *(Scitex Continuous Tone). For transferring images between Scitex imaging equipment and desktop computer systems and applications (such as Photoshop).*

.SEA (*Self-Extracting Archive). A compression format that may be generated by several applications, including Stuffit and Disk Doubler. Useful for sending files, which can be opened at their destination with a mouse-click, without decompression software.*

SYLK *(Symbolic Link). Allows transfer of numerical data; used by spreadsheet applications, such as Excel.*

TARGA *(Truevision Targa). Used with PC systems equipped with an appropriate video board, in video applications that allow a graphic image to be overlaid on a video frame.*

TIFF *(Tagged Information File Format). Bitmapped graphic files of varying resolution, for use with both color and black-and-white scanned or electronically created images. Commonly used as Save format for image-editing programs or scans. Useful for exchanging files between Mac and PC platforms. Offers LZW compression option. Windows extension: .TIF.*

Windows Extensions. *A dot and a three-character file extension must accompany all PC file names (which are limited to eight characters, for example: BROCHURE.DOC). The extension specifies the file type. Graphics file extensions would use the types noted here, such as .EPS, .TIF, or .JPG.*

WKS *(Worksheet). For transferring files to some PC spreadsheet applications.*

How to save a Mac file to a different format

With the file open, select Save As from the File menu. Look for a file format selection menu. If one is available, choose the format you want to save to; for example, saving from a MS Word format to an RTF format. Type a name for the new file, keeping in mind the file's destinations. For instance, PC file names are limited to eight characters with a three-character extension, such as NEWTEXT1.DOC.

Using EPS and TIFF files

EPS file format and its uses

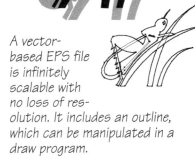

EPS (Encapsulated PostScript) is the format of choice for object-oriented (vector-based) PostScript graphic files, such as those generated by Freehand, Corel Draw, or other draw programs. It is also the necessary format for Photoshop duotones and clipping paths.

A vector-based EPS file is infinitely scalable with no loss of resolution. It includes an outline, which can be manipulated in a draw program.

Advantages: Vector-based images can be scaled to any size with no loss of quality, and individual objects can be selected and altered. Vector-based file sizes tend to be relatively small. The images require little memory to process. EPS files can be used cross-platform, but require all linked files, such as fonts or placed graphics files, to be available.

Disadvantages: A PostScript printer is required for output; a PostScript application is required for editing. Bitmap EPS files tend to be very large. Bitmap images decrease in output quality and show pixellation if they are enlarged beyond their usable resolution. "Nested" EPS files or vector images with too many control points can cause output problems.

Adobe Streamline can trace bitmap images and convert them to EPS/PostScript-editable graphics. Experiment with conversion settings and be prepared for some detail loss and a harder-edged look.

A quick way to transfer EPS images

Not all applications can utilize EPS images directly; notably, some word processors cannot. You can convert the EPS to a PICT format in an image-processing application. On the Mac, it is quicker to use the Clipboard. Open the PostScript file you want to transfer and select the image, then press the Option key as you use the Copy command. This places a PICT version onto the Clipboard. Now you can paste the image into your word processing document.

TIFF file format and its uses

TIFF is the preferred format for grayscale images.

TIFF is the preferred format for bitmap image files, such as those generated with image-editing software (Photoshop, Painter, CorelPaint), or for scanned images. Bitmapped images may be saved as EPS files, but they will retain bitmap characteristics and editing requirements. An EPS file can be five to twenty times as large as a TIFF file, to no advantage. Exception: a Photoshop image containing a clipping path, duotone information, or APR (automatic picture replacement) compatibility must be saved as an EPS file.

Advantages: TIFF images can output on any printer. They transfer easily between platforms, and are compatible with a wide range of applications. The LZW compression option often produces much smaller file sizes.

Disadvantages: Bitmapped images decrease in output quality and show pixellation if they are enlarged beyond their usable resolution. Resizing can also produce moiré patterns. Fix this by scaling images to even multiples of your printer's dpi (example: for a 600 dpi printer, 20% would work; 17% could cause problems). Bitmaps also require more memory to process.

Avoiding TIFF file problems

Never place a TIFF image with Background None specified in the picture box. The resulting image will have ragged edges. For a full-frame image, specify a background the color of the page against which the image will appear (specify white for an unprinted background area). If you want the image outlined against the background, create a clipping path in the image file. If you simply want the image as an FPO or to swap out in APR, "Background None" is okay, but avoid "auto image" type runarounds; the text won't flow properly. Instead, use a polygon picture box to control the runaround.

Use TIFF format for scanned line art.

When saving a TIFF image, you can reduce the file size up to 50% by choosing the LZW file compression option. However, do not use this option if the file is to be output as a live image on a Scitex PS/2 RIP; this equipment cannot read LZW compressed files.

Vector-based (draw program) art, duotones, and CMYK images need to be saved in EPS format. It is best to make a separate file for each EPS graphic, rather than "ganging" several on one page, which can cause output problems.

A bitmap image shows pixellation when enlarged beyond its usable resolution range.

A TIFF image may display jagged edges when its picture box has a background color of None and is superimposed over a tint.

Specifying a background color of white (or a spot color) prevents pixellated edges.

Another way to ensure sharp edges on an outlined image: save it with a clipping path. Save the image as an EPS in Photoshop.

File compression

Whether you are running out of hard disk space, archiving large files, or sending files by modem, file compression is a useful tool. You can double your storage space and greatly hasten the copying or transmission process. Compression software takes various forms, from simple shrinking of individual files (which Stuffit does admirably) to sophisticated archiving programs (like Now Utilities). Some, like AutoDoubler, operate transparently to increase available hard disk space (test these on your system for possible conflicts). Many of these transparent programs offer idle-time compression, allowing your computer to compress and archive files unattended, while you sleep. Some programs (notably image-editing applications) offer built-in compression options. Assess your needs and shop around.

When you transmit compressed files for use by others, be sure that they can be decompressed at the other end. One way to ensure this is to compress the file as a self-extracting archive, or .sea. It will decompress, ready for use, with a double-click.

Another considerate precaution is to use proper extensions, so recipients will be able to decompress without having to guess what type of file they are dealing with. DropRename is a simple and extremely useful Mac program that allows the user to rename files in batches, as when file types change.

Lossy vs. lossless

There are two types of compression: lossy and lossless. Lossy compression discards redundant data during compression; it is used primarily on picture, sound, and video files. Due to data loss, quality reduction can vary with file type and software. Lossless retains all data, and is used exclusively for such files as word processing or databases, where data retention is critical. The compression is correspondingly less.

Identifying compressed files

You may receive compressed files occasionally, as from an online service, shrunk in a format you don't recognize. Your computer may give you the message that it can't find the application to open the file. Compressed files often include a filename extension (a three-letter suffix), which identifies the compression program. Once you know this, you can hunt down the program (many are available on-line as shareware) or try opening it with Stuffit.

Common file extensions

Extension	program/format
.BIN	Stuffit
.CPT	Compact Pro
.DD	DiskDoubler
f	Diamond
.HQX	BinHex, Stuffit
.PAK	PakWorks
.PIT	Packit
.PKG	AppleLink
.s, .x	SuperDisk!
.SEA	Self-extracting archive
.SIT	Stuffit
.zip	PC compression using WinZip or PKZip

Working cross-platform and cross-application

Cross-platform issues

Most office applications (word processors, databases, spreadsheets) have file formats that open documents fairly seamlessly between Mac and PC versions. Some have built-in utilities that handle the conversion; the same is true of commonly used page layout programs. However, some of the material (such as placed images and fonts) within the transferred document may not translate as desired. Also, opening and working on documents both cross-platform and cross-application can pose some problems. Some forethought is necessary. Run some tests before you find that you have committed to an impossible situation with a deadline attached!

File exchange

Exchanging files between Mac and PC platforms can be expedited by observing a few protocols.

On the Mac end: if you are running System 7.5, you have a PC translator built into your system; you can insert a 3.5-inch PC floppy disc, copy files, and rename them. If you are running an earlier system software, a program called Apple File Exchange (which is included with the Mac's system disks) needs to be installed and launched before the PC disk is inserted. Apple also sells a control panel application called PC Exchange, which offers more options. It renames Mac files so they are readable by a PC, while retaining the original name for the Mac. Floppy disks can be formatted and files copied according to their destination system.

When preparing files on the Mac for use on a PC, use the PC option when you format the floppy that will contain the files; this will make the translation smoother.

Exchanging text files between platforms and applications

To retain most or all of the formatting as well as the text itself, first determine which word processor will be used by the person receiving the file, and save in that format. Using the RTF file format for text will keep most of the information intact between platforms and applications. This format retains the text styling, tabs, and other qualities inherent in the document, and translates fairly seamlessly between applications and platforms. If you are on the file-receiving end, furnish information on the file's destination (which programs it will be used with) to the person sending you the file, and request that it be saved in an appropriate format. To hedge your bet, have it saved in several formats; one will probably work!

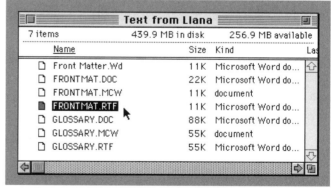

If you are receiving a text file from someone, ask for it in the format of the software edition you are using: for example, if you plan to bring the document into MS Word, request that the file be saved as an MS Word file. Also, Word 6.0's filters can read most other text formats.

To open the text file on the Mac: Launch your word processor. Choose Open from the File menu, choosing the most general setting in the popup menu (such as All Documents in Word). If the PC file shows in the Open File box, double-click on its name; it should convert to your word processor's format.

If all else fails, request the file in plain text or ASCII form. This will just give you the unformatted, plain text, but at least all the typing will be done and your word processor will definitely be able to open the file! Always request a hard copy printout of a sender's text file. That way, if you have to resort to ASCII, you'll still have a text styling reference.

To save some headaches when working with a PC-generated text file on the Mac, ask that returns be used only on paragraphs, and not on each line. It is often best to apply your own styles (such as bold, italic) to text so that you can specify the correct typeface, rather than a keystroke-generated style. This can be done easily with style sheets. You may want to ask your correspondent to leave out styles altogether.

Keystroke encoding may be inconsistent between the Mac and PC, causing some formatting codes or special characters (bullets, fractions, accents, etc.) to be lost or garbled. If this happens, you will simply have to fix the text. A quick way to replace special characters: use the Find/Replace command on the translated document. Converting the text to No Style, then applying style sheets, may help, too.

Fonts and text

Exchanging PostScript fonts cross-platform holds the potential for font ID problems. Be aware of the names for both screen and printer (outline) fonts to be used; they may look the same on screen, but, if named differently, may not output correctly.

Placed graphics

Macs use PICT resource files to display EPS images on screen; PCs use TIFF. This means that EPS images embedded in cross-platform files will display differently, or not at all. Although they output correctly, sizing and cropping a gray tint instead of a photo representation could be challenging at least. It would be best, where possible, to do all such image manipulation before making the translation.

Another workaround is to use TIFF images between platforms, when clipping paths are not needed. The catch: TIFF files do not behave the same in all cross-platform conditions; not all PC illustration programs can read Mac TIFFs. A fix: use Photoshop as a translator, to save the TIFF in a Mac or PC-friendly format. Always use the .TIF file extension for cross-platform TIFF files.

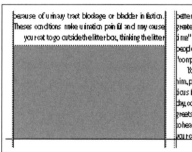

Sizing and cropping an irregularly shaped image is very difficult if a screen representation is not available.

Importing a TIFF image may provide the necessary visual aid.

Design & Layout Tips
Traditional vs. digital methods

One of the great advantages of computer-generated art is the time (and therefore money) saved in its production. Changes and duplications may take only a mouse click. Multiple elements can be brought together easily; the initial concept may quickly become the final product. However, there are cases in which you are better off using non-electronic media and techniques. For instance, you may wish to create a brushstroke pattern that would require skills or software you don't possess, or would simply require more time to generate electronically than traditionally. In such a case, it would make sense simply to scan hand-drawn art. Or you may want a printed effect that would be awkward or time-consuming to achieve by your own manipulation of digital art, but that could be achieved very simply at the stripping stage of film production.

Some tasks for which the computer clearly has the edge are page layout, technical drawing, photo retouching and manipulation, three-dimensional rendering, presentations, animation, and multimedia projects. Other areas that are more of a judgment call are freehand drawing and calligraphy and conventional (as opposed to digital) photography. In some cases, a combination of approaches may work best.

A good rule of thumb: when you are spending more time seeking workarounds than actually completing the job, it is time to look at other options.

Doing it yourself vs. outsourcing

It is important to assess the realities of the job, your abilities, and your equipment's capabilities honestly. Do you really have the time and skills to scan, adjust, retouch, and color-correct an image, or would it be more cost-effective to have the printer shoot a negative, prepare it, and strip in the film (or send you a low-resolution file for placement in your page layout)?

Thinking through the process before you begin and familiarity with the resources at hand will guide your choice of the most effective method, saving time and aggravation. Keep in mind Murphy's Law of electronic publishing: your disk may crash just when your deadline looms close. It's a good idea to have some backup resources handy.

The truth is, unless you have unlimited purchasing resources and unlimited time to learn all the tools, you will never be completely on top of the technological wave. You need to do what creative people have always done: find solutions to problems with the means available.

Combining traditional and electronic page layout methods

The best graphic technique is often a mix of both traditional (manual) and electronic media; the most effective and expedient mix is up to your best judgment. Here are some suggestions for combining sketches and software to retain the looseness of hand-drawn layout while achieving the finished look of electronic design.

Start with a black-and-white version of your layout to keep it simple, and to define the basic elements on the page. Once your composition is to your liking, add color if you wish.

Working at 30 to 50% of final size, sketch a number of thumbnail roughs of your page, combining type, photo, and graphic elements. Scan your favorite sketch, saving the scan as a 72 dpi TIFF file (the standard resolution of an image viewed on a monitor).

In your page layout software, import the TIFF file into a picture box the size of your finished page for use as a "tracing template." Reduce the shade of the image to about 30% so it will not overpower the type and guidelines you lay over it. This trick also works well when duplicating or revising an existing page layout if you have only a printed sample to work from; you can match spacing and style exactly.

With the "template" in place, build your layout over it, adding type, picture boxes, alignment guides, and any other imported graphics you want to use. Experiment with type specifications, striving to maintain the look and feel of your original sketch.

Once you have created your layout over the tracing template, you can cut the template from its box. You may want to keep some graphic elements from your sketch as placeholders; if so, simply duplicate the window, resize it to frame those elements, and position them as you wish. You might want to assign a type runaround to an image, so that type will wrap around it.

You can now print out your layout, both for your own appraisal and as a first draft to show your client. If text is in place, you can use this as a proofreading copy.

To get a fair comparison with your original thumbnail sketch, try printing your layout in thumbnail mode by checking that option in the Print dialog box.

Layout tips

How to align page elements easily

To quickly match your page layout to an existing printed document without taking measurements, scan the printed page at 300 dpi and save as a TIFF. Bring the TIFF into your page layout and screen it back or colorize it, then use it as a template to build the page around. Check a laser print-out of the resulting file on a light table against the original. When you are satisfied, discard the TIFF from the file and save. This is especially handy for forms.

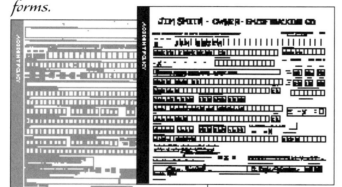

Checking your layout

When viewing a page layout on screen, turn off the guides now and then to evaluate the composition.

When you design a form or a piece requiring cuts and folds, always print out and construct a dummy to make sure it fits your specs, and to serve as a guide for the printer/binder.

Three ways to figure photo proportions

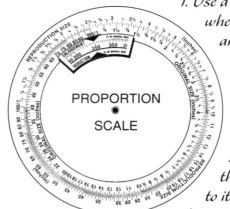

1. Use a proportion wheel, available at art supply stores. You line up the tic marks on two concentric circles, matching the measurements of the original photo to its reproduction dimensions (the window it will fit into). The result is a percentage of the original size, shown in a window on the wheel.

2. Use a calculator. Divide the width of your photo

window by the width of the original photo (use the chart on page 49 to convert to decimals). The result is a percentage enlargement or reduction. To determine the reproduction height of the photo, multiply the height of the original by the percentage.

3. Use software, like Designsoft's Prowheel, to do your calculations on the desktop.

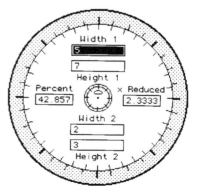

Shortcuts for pages using graphics

Screen redraws of pages containing complex graphics can slow you down. To speed up your work, try turning off the on-screen display; many applications have a command for this. You will see a gray box instead of the image.

If you find that your page prints out too slowly (or not at all), try using low-res images as just described. Where the art incorporates complex fills, save a simplified placeholder version and use it to print with. When ready for final output, update the page layout file with the full versions of the art.

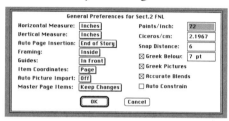

Quark's picture display suppression command shows pictures as gray boxes until individually selected.

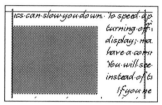 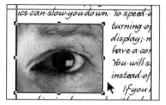

If you need to see the graphics in place, work with a low-resolution version of the image file. Save a 72 dpi version of the original image file and use it FPO (for position only). Give it the same name as the original file, and store it in a different folder. When it is time to output the page, send the high-res version along with the page file. The imagesetter will substitute the high-resolution original for the low-res placeholder.

Gradient fills slow down screen redraws, too; for speed, use a solid fill until you have finished other work on the file, adding the gradient fill as the final step.

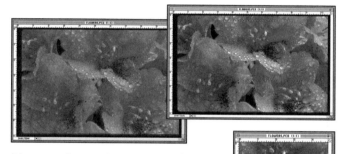

You can shave a bitmap image's size by cropping it and sizing it in its original file, rather than in the page layout application.

When you place an image in a bordered rectangular picture box, make sure there is a little bit extra all around the cropping area. It may look as if it fills the box on the monitor, but if it is even a bit too small, you will get a white line between photo and box border when it prints.

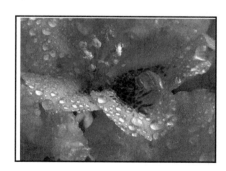

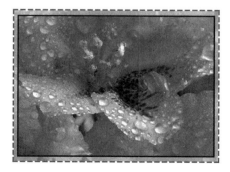

Measuring and dividing page layouts and artwork

If your application does not provide the measurement scale you need, make your own. One way is  to scan the ruler of your choice at 100%, save it as a TIFF, and bring it into the document you are working on as a layer or separate picture element. Use it to line up the other elements as desired, then delete it from the file.

To divide a page into equal sections vertically, create a type box in your page layout application. Make it the width of the space you want to divide. Set the number of columns for the number of divisions you need, and set the gutter width to the smallest increment available in the program. You can now draw guidelines matched to the column dividers, and delete the type box.

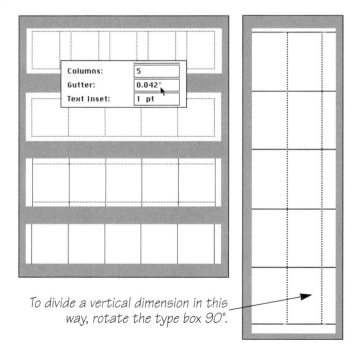

To divide a vertical dimension in this way, rotate the type box 90°.

Using a grid to compose the page

If you produce a publication at regular intervals, set up a grid template to expedite page layout. A grid is a visual framework in which you arrange text, photos, and graphic elements. It lends consistency throughout the publication and saves time by giving you a ready-made layout guide.

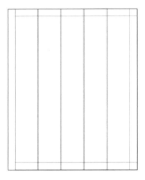
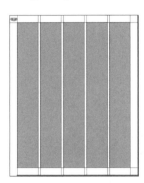

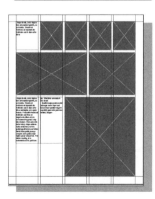

Five-column grids offer great flexibility and interesting balance. A scholar's margin (an outside column left open to receive text or graphics) can hold headlines, cutlines, pull-quotes, graphics, or white space.

How to make your own registration marks

From time to time, you will need to place your own registration, crop, or fold marks in a document rather than using the default marks from the application. Your trim size may be smaller than the selected page size, or you may want to gang elements on a page (a way to save money at the service bureau). Registration and crop marks permit graphic elements from different sources to be stripped together accurately.

To make a registration mark in a page layout program, create a circle with a ¼" diameter and a border width of .5 point. Using guides for perfect alignment, make .5 point crosshairs intersecting the center of the circle.

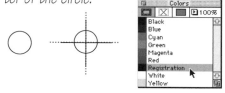

Color these objects "Registration" from the color palette, and group them.

To make a registration mark in a draw program, make the circle and crosshair combination, group it, and copy it, centering each one over the other and coloring each with a color to be used in the document. For a four-color process graphic, you would have black, cyan, magenta, and yellow marks, respectively. Then group them all (see page 81, fig. 1).

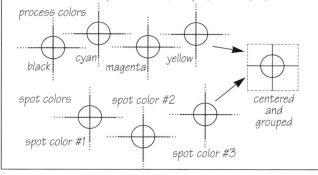

process colors

black   cyan   magenta   yellow

spot colors   spot color #2   centered and grouped

spot color #1   spot color #3

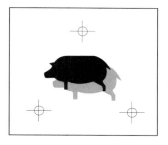

Place the mark at several locations just outside the live area of your page or graphic. A registration mark will print out for each color used in the document.

These registration marks are useful when printing out separations on a laser printer to check alignment.

When setting up a page document that will contain

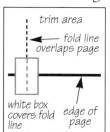

trim area

fold line overlaps page

white box covers fold line   edge of page

multiple folds or unusual folds or cuts, you may need to include fold marks to guide the printer/binder. To create these marks, draw a dashed line .5 points in width and ½" long. Select black as its color (or whatever single custom color is to be printed). Position the line so that it overlaps the trim area of your page . Next, make a small box, color it white, and place it at the edge of the trim line, covering the dotted fold line. Your fold mark will print out, but won't show inside the trim area.

To make crop marks, make a set of guidelines ⅛" apart, at right angles. Set the application to Snap to

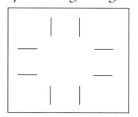

Guides. Draw a dashed line .5 points in width and ½" long. Select black (or the predominat ink) as its color. Duplicate it, and place the copy at right angles. Position these lines so that they butt to the outermost guides, and group them. Duplicate them, then create two mirror images. You now have a full set of crop marks, which can be positioned at the corners of any size image, 1/8" outside the trim area.

Save these marks in a folder for later use.

Making mockups and comps

When using a black-and-white laser printer, print out the colored areas of a layout as a low percentage of black, then color them with marker or colored pencil. The screened-back area will serve as a guide, but will not show up under the added color.

You can use a metallic marker to simulate metallic ink or a foil stamp. A more realistic but costly tool is Pantone's Omnichrom, which adheres areas of color to black toner using a special heat applicator. There are hand-held and tabletop models.

Using "greeking"

If you need to comp a page with text areas, but don't have the actual copy yet, use "greeking" to indicate the text. It will show the type style and format without calling undue attention to the faked wording.

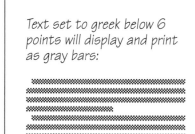

Text set to greek below 6 points will display and print as gray bars:

An alternate way to "greek" body type: set your application to greek text at a higher point size than the text you plan to use; it will print out as gray bars to indicate the text area.

To make your own "greek" text file, type or scan these sample paragraphs—or a passage of your choice—into a word processing program and save them as a template file, copying and pasting to fill any given text area.

Lorem ipsum dolor sit amet, consecteur adpiscing elit, sed diam nonnumy elusmod tempor incidune ut labore. Edrepudiand sint er moletsia non recusand. Italqu sarens it luptat pelenoir ellfic. Tia non ab se solu Incommod quase egenium.

Polendium caritat preasert coum omining null sit ause pecandl quartt in emigent cupidat a naturea proficis facile explent sine julla unrea. Invitat igitur vera ratio bene sanos ad coercend magis and et dodese endesse ideantur. Invitat igfitur vere quea egnium inreob fugiended. Tia non obeasolu incommod.

Atque ut odia, invid despication adversantur luptabib, sic amiciantia. Non modo fautriscsa ad alperasiti ate fidelissim sed al etiam effertirice sunt luptan amic quam busnon. Preasentib fruunt sed fidelissim sed firma et. dequib ante ditum est, sic amicitanmd beg posse a luptate discdere. Nam cum sokitud er vitary. Atque ectamen nedue emim hanc movere potest appetit amim ned ullam habet ictum pellat peccage eronylar at ille pellit sensar luptae epicur semper hot. For natura expeting ea in motuoiumn sit ille pellit sensar. What tirur convente ab alia dicert.

Busdam neque pecan modut est nequa nonor imper ned honor imper epuular religard cupiditat, quas nulla praid om undant. Impprob pary minuit.

Amdoi, arotat radser ci, pomog smi dot cais eccams qierto om e, ogemt ciodat a matira rofocos facote exemt some kis.

How to get richer CMYK blacks

Specifying a 100% black can produce a washed-out black in CMYK. To obtain deeper, richer solid black areas in four-color process, try this formula: 60% cyan, 40% magenta, 20% yellow, 100% black.

Using this formula will also prevent show-through of other colors when a black area is over-printed. Adjust your percentages so that the total combination of overprinting process black and underlying tint add up to 300% or less, the upper limit of ink coverage for most presses. For example: a black composed of 60C, 40M, 20Y, 100K over-printing a tint of 30M, 100Y totals 350%, too much coverage. Changing the black formula to 20C, 20M, 20Y, 100K totals 290 when combined with the 30M, 100Y tint, an acceptable ink coverage.

You can also produce a "warmer" or a "cooler" black by varying the percentages of cyan, magenta, and yellow. For a cool "rich black," try 30% cyan with 100% black; for a warmer black, substitute 30% magenta for cyan (see page 81, fig. 2). Avoid heavier ink percentages to prevent too heavy an ink coverage.

Making bar codes

It can be a great convenience to create your own bar codes for placement in package designs, book covers, and labels. Bar-code software, available for both Macs and PCs, enables you to create bar-code graphics without leaving your page layout, word processor, or database program. Synex Bar Code Pro produces EPS bar code files; Azalea software includes fonts and Quark extensions for bar code creation.

Use care to ensure that the final printed version of the bar code will scan correctly at warehouse or checkout counter. Never use scanned original bar code art as live art in a page layout; either generate the bar code art from software or have the printer strip in an original film negative from a reliable source. To be doubly sure before the press run, have a high-resolution proof of the bar code scanned by the type of equipment it will be exposed to in actual use (take it to your local supermarket or book-store). You may also want to have it tested with verification equipment, which will measure its readability against industry standards.

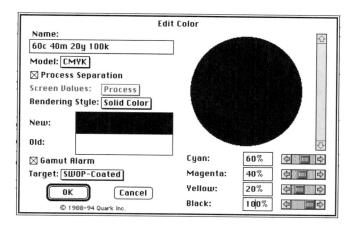

How to avoid problems with gradient fills

Choose colors carefully when creating blends. Use neighboring colors (such as green and yellow) and avoid complementary colors to avoid muddy blends—unless you want that effect (see page 81, fig. 3). Avoid blends between spot colors or between spot and process colors; these are very difficult to trap. Instead, blend a spot color to a lighter tint of that color. When blending a spot color to white, specify 0% of the spot color, not white.

Banding is a potential problem with blends destined for print. PostScript RIP devices, which process only 256 shades of gray, are technically incapable of producing "perfect" gradients longer than 7 inches. This applies to each color channel. When the range of tones is interrupted by abrupt tonal shifts, banding is the result. It occurs in process color, but can be more pronounced in single-color printing. Any vignette longer than 7 1/2" will probably involve some banding, especially if generated by a page layout or drawing program. Photoshop or other bitmap image processing programs create better gradients, and allow "noise" and blurring to be added, permitting an unlimited number of dots in the tint area and more subtle effects. For best results, a graphic file should contain no more than ten blends.

To predict the probability of banding, use this formula for each color channel:

$$(\text{beginning \%} - \text{ending \%}) \times (\text{dpi}/\text{lpi})^2 = \text{number of shades}$$

Example: a fill ranging from 100% to 0% black printed on a 1,200 dpi imagesetter using a 150-line halftone screen would have 64 shades of gray.

To compute the change rate of the shades, divide the number of shades by the distance covered. If the above example covered 72 points (1"), then the rate of change would be one shade per .88 point. The ideal rate is around one shade per point, but certain colors may allow slightly higher rates. For example, a cyan channel changing at one shade per point may mask a coarser change in yellow (say, one shade per 10 points).

The order of perceptibility from least to most is yellow, cyan, magenta, black. Black increases the risk of banding. Banding is intensified by using the same range of percentages in two or more color channels. Lower the risk by decreasing the size of the gradient area, increasing the percentage range, raising the dpi, or lowering the lpi.

Page layout program

Vector-based draw program

Image-processing program

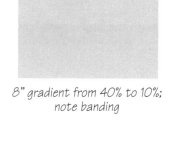
8" gradient from 40% to 10%; note banding

Avoiding "shade-stepping"

When a blend created in a draw program contains too few steps between shades, banding can occur. To figure the number of steps to use in such a blend, use this equation:

$$\left(\frac{\text{printer resolution (dpi)}}{\text{screen frequency (lpi)}}\right)^2 = \text{approximate number of shades available}$$

The result of the calculation tells you the approximate number of pixels in each halftone dot produced by the printer.

On a 300 dpi printer set at 60 lpi, each halftone dot is composed of a grid of approximately $(300/60)^2$, or 25 pixels. This means that you have 25 possible shades to work with, plus one more white shade, totaling 26 steps.

Using the maximum printer resolution makes available the maximum number of shades or tint sections.

Increasing the screen frequency without increasing the resolution will give fewer tint sections.

Although you can sometimes eliminate shade-stepping by decreasing screen frequency, you also get larger halftone dots and a coarser screen. Increasing the number of steps in your blend will not compensate for higher screen frequency; the steps aren't available.

When blending process color tints, identify the largest percentage color change between CMYK values. For example, a blend from 10%Y /50%M to 80%Y/70%M would mean a 70% change, indicated by the change in yellow.

Use the table below to figure quickly how many steps to use in a blend. First, determine what percentage change in color you will be making. Then find the appropriate row and column, based on the dpi and lpi to be used.

Blending from black to white on a 1270 dpi printer: a 100% change needs 200 steps. A 50% change, as from 20% black to 70% black, needs 100 steps.

Resolutions dpi	300	400	600	1270		2540		
Screen Frequencies lpi	60	60	75	90	120	120	133	150
Percent Change								
10%	3	5	7	20	11	45	36	29
20%	5	9	13	40	22	90	73	57
30%	8	14	20	60	34	135	109	86
40%	10	18	26	80	45	179	146	115
50%	13	23	32	100	56	224	182	143
60%	15	27	39	120	67	269	218	172
70%	18	32	45	140	78	313	255	201
80%	20	36	52	160	90	358	292	229
90%	23	41	58	180	101	403	328	258
100%	25	45	64	200	112	448	365	287

Number of Steps Needed in Blend

Text, Fonts, & Typography
Font management

To save space on your hard drive, keep only those fonts you are currently using and those you use continually in documents. Deactivated fonts and fonts stored outside the system fonts folder promote quicker startup and opening of applications because fewer fonts will be loading. Keep the rest archived and ready for use on a separate storage medium.

Various utilities, including Adobe Type Reunion, MenuFonts, and Suitcase display fonts in selection menus as the actual typefaces.

Adobe Type Manager (ATM) is the requisite utility for working with PostScript fonts. It allows accurate screen representation of type, and also permits certain

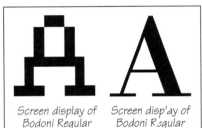

Screen display of Bodoni Regular without ATM

Screen display of Bodoni Regular with ATM

type effects in various applications. It also influences the way type prints on a PostScript printer.

```
☐ Galliard family
☐ Garamond family
☐ Gill Sans family
☐ Goudy family
☐ Helv Inserat
☐ Helvetica family
☐ Impact family
☐ Italia family
☐ Kabel family
```

Print out a menu of the fonts you have, so you can locate them quickly.

Use a font-management utility like Suitcase or Master Juggler to organize and control your fonts. Create a suitcase of frequently used fonts as your startup set, keeping it to a manageable size, and deactivating the rest. You can add temporary sets or sets designated for specific jobs, as needed.

To help the utility load and manage your fonts, create a filing system for font suitcases. For example, group fonts by type foundry (Monotype, Adobe, Fonthaus), characteristics (serif, san serif, display, ornate), or any system that enables you to search and find them easily.

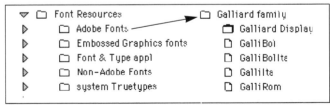

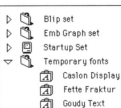

You can speed up your computer's operations by organizing your fonts and using a font-managing utility to group them and selectively turn them on and off.

Font identification
Mac fonts are found in the System folder:

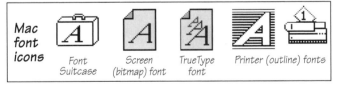

Mac font icons	Font Suitcase	Screen (bitmap) font	TrueType font	Printer (outline) fonts

Windows font extensions
.ttf   TrueType Font
.pfb   PostScript Font File (binary)
.pfa   PostScript Font File (ascii)

Working with text and fonts

Converting type to outlines

To avoid missing-font problems with files generated in draw programs, convert all text to outlines (paths) before saving the file for output. This also helps to prevent PostScript errors. You will find the command under the Type menus in Freehand and Illustrator. It is a good idea to save a version with unconverted text, for editing the file later. (Type converted to outlines changes from editable type to a vector-based object.)

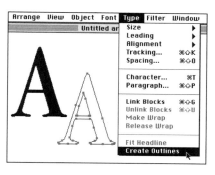

Working with style sheets and text

Make your text styles easier to find in their pop-up dialog box. Begin their names with a number, such as: 1Headline, 2Subhead, 3Body Text, 4Caption, and so on. This way, they are stacked in order of usage.

Proofreading

Proofreading is best done with hard copy, but here is a good on-screen proofreading trick.

Change the entire document's text color to blue. As you proofread, change the proofed text to red; that way, you will always know where you left off. When editing, add new text in a different color, so that it can be isolated and checked. Variations on this include assigning a different color to each proofreader. You can color-code Find and Replace operations. Finding colored section heads is much easier. Colors can be built into style sheet definitions and formatting instructions, too.

The read-aloud feature in Apple's SimpleText can be a great proofreading tool: import the copy you want to proof into SimpleText, and have it read it back to you as you proof hard copy!

You only need one copy of SimpleText on your drive, however; trash all those copies that came bundled with other software, along with TeachText, the older version.

> Notify the person providing your text file not to use space-bars instead of tabs, not to use hard returns except at the beginnings of paragraphs (and to use only ONE), and not to use tabs when you want indents, including hanging indents.
>
> Typists tend to use double spaces after periods. If you receive such a file, use Find / Replace to change double to single spaces.

Take advantage of a word processor's capabilities to prep text before importing it to your page layout. For instance, use Microsoft Word's Case command to specify upper or lower case on sections of text. Alphabetizing a list takes a keystroke in Word.

Be sure that you have the Symbol font installed. Some printer drivers use information stored in the font to print out special characters in downloadable fonts.

Do not change the names of PostScript fonts; the printer won't be able to find them and will substitute a different font, usually `Courier`.

TrueType fonts

TrueType icon

Although TrueType fonts may offer some advantages when used for monitor display, they tend to be problematic when used in high-end systems for output. Service bureaus and printers do not like them and frequently advise against them, citing font identification conflicts and faulty output. It is better practice to use PostScript fonts in all documents intended for output to film, plates, or proofs from a high-end system.

Typography tips

Using type effectively

❖ Serif typefaces are generally considered the most readable choice for body text.
Examples: Times Roman, Bookman, Garamond, **Bodoni**, Cheltenham

❖ Sans serif type is a good choice for headlines and short phrases, especially where space is limited.
Examples: **Helvetica Inserat,** Gill Sans, **Futura Condensed,** Eras, Kabel Medium

❖ *USING ALL CAPS IN BODY TEXT BECOMES MONOTONOUS, HARD TO READ, AND EVENTUALLY OBNOXIOUS.*

❖ Two typeface families are usually sufficient in a document.
Example: Gill Sans heads, Garamond text

❖ **Italic and bold text should be used sparingly to create emphasis; otherwise, nothing is emphasized;** *however, they are generally preferable to* underlines.

❖ Consider your readership.
Point sizes below 8 are difficult for many people to read.

❖ Avoid very wide and very narrow column widths for most body text. An alphabet and a half (about 40 characters) column width is traditionally considered optimal, but it really depends on the typeface, point size, and desired effect.

❖ Suit the personality of the type to the tone of the document.

❖ Since most computer typefaces are proportionally spaced (with exceptions such as monospaced `Chicago` or `Courier`), extra spaces after periods are unnecessary. Get rid of them by doing a Find/Replace command, replacing double spaces with single.

Ligatures

Ligatures can add grace and readability to your serif text. To create them:

	Mac keystrokes	PC keystrokes
æ	*Option/ '*	*ALT/0230*
Æ	*Option/Shift/ '*	*ALT/0198*
œ	*Option/q*	*ALT/0156*
Œ	*Option/Shift/q*	*ALT/0140*
fi	*Option/Shift/5*	—
fl	*Option/Shift/6*	—

You can add them to your text by using the Find/Replace command.

Use printer's ornaments and dingbats, available as fonts from several vendors, to separate text sections.

❀ They make interesting alternatives to bullets.

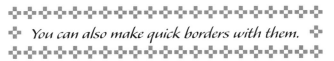

❖ You can also make quick borders with them.

Headlines

Headlines should draw the reader into the page while harmonizing with the rest of the page elements. When in doubt, try a different version of the text face in a larger point size (roughly 150 to 200% text size), such as Poster Bodoni with Bodoni Roman.

Headlines require more attention to kerning, leading, and line length than body text.

Generally, heads are best set flush left; however, different alignments can set different tones (as with centered mixed caps and small caps for a formal look).

Smaller heads work well if allowed plenty of space on the page.

Small caps

Small caps have visibly different weights from normal caps. If this is visually awkward in your layout, create the headline type in a draw program and stroke the small cap characters with black (or the full caps with white) to make their weights compatible.

Printing character sets

The Type Book is shareware, available online, which will print out type samples for you in various formats. You can use it to make a looseleaf directory of fonts for quick reference.

Matching typefaces

When called upon to identify and match a typeface, look for key characters to match up. Each typeface has certain characters that are especially unique to it, such as the lowercase f, a, e, and g. Study the parts of several characters and compare these details.

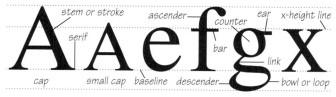

Typeface anatomy

Bookman Cheltenham Garamond Bodoni Palatino Stone Serif

Helvetica Futura Stone Sans Eras Kabel Gill Sans

Lowercase g's wide variety of forms is a useful font identifier.

QUICK BROWN FOX

Headline set in page layout software, using the small caps command. Notice the difference in stroke weight between the large and small caps.

QUICK BROWN FOX

The same headline, set in a draw program. The small caps were set in a smaller point size and given a 1.25 point black stroke, to match the weight of the large caps. Some fonts, notably expert sets, include true small caps.

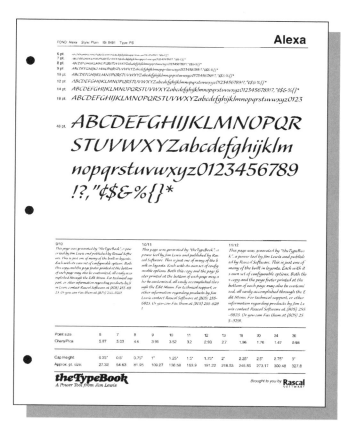

A sample type specimen page, printed out from The Type Book. The full alphabet of the font is displayed, along with several sample paragraphs and copyfitting specifications.

Making updatable text

How to use a special black plate for updating text

When laying out a publication containing text that will be translated or otherwise altered in subsequent versions, create a second black spot color with a unique name (such as Text Black) in the page layout file. Apply this color, manually or by inclusion in a style sheet, to any text that will be altered. This way, only one new plate of film for each altered page will need to be output; it can be stripped with the existing color plates for a new press run.

You can make a text-editable black-and-white screen shot by assigning it to a Text Black printing plate. Open the color TIFF file in Photoshop and convert it to grayscale mode. Then convert the grayscale TIFF to a Monotone by selecting Duotone (under Mode) and assigning a custom color, called Text Black, composed of 0% cyan, 0% magenta, 0% yellow, and 100% black. Save as an EPS file. Check your page layout to be sure the image imports correctly. You can then output the image on the same plate as other designated Text Black text.

Adding readable and correctable text over a color photo

Try this tip for overprinting black text on a color bitmapped image. Begin with an RGB background image in Photoshop. Set Black Generation to None in the Separation Setup dialog box under Preferences, then convert the image to CMYK. This will leave an empty black channel in the image. Using Photoshop's controls, lighten the image so that black text will be easily readable when superimposed on the background image. The black text should be set to overprint in whatever application was used to generate it. In this way, changes and corrections involving only the black printing plate may be made to the text. This technique works best with high-value images that do not depend on black for shadow definition (see page 81, fig.4).

How to create reversed type

Reversed type (type "knocking out" of an ink color to print the color of the paper) can easily be created in a draw or page layout program. Simply select the text and specify it as white. Specifying another color or tint produces type that reverses out of an area of darker color, but contains a fill of a lighter color. For readability, use this judiciously. For example, type reversed out of black and filled with yellow is highly readable; filled with red, the same type will be illegible (see page 81, fig. 5).

To create more complex reverses

In a draw program, use the Scissors or Knife tool to cut the line of type in half. Join the free ends of each half and fill each half with a different color or pattern. For very complex type, you may need to create two differently filled versions, stack them, and create a mask for the top one. It may also be necessary to convert the type to outlines first.

In Illustrator (the procedure is much the same in Freehand), create the text you want to reverse out. Select the text and specify a fill and stroke, if desired (in this case, 70% black fill and .5-point white stroke). With the type selected, choose the Copy command, then the Paste In Front command. With the copy selected, specify a different fill (30% here, with the same .5-point stroke).

Draw a rectangle over the lower half of the text (for a straight line reversal) or an irregular shape (for a curved line), making sure to cover the lower half of the type. Specify a fill and stroke of None. Select both the top text copy and the rectangle, and use the Group command. Choose the Make Mask command. Add a dark background behind the type.

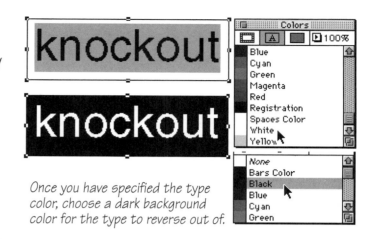

Once you have specified the type color, choose a dark background color for the type to reverse out of.

For a more complex reverse effect, text is set in Illustrator, with a 70% black fill and .5 point white stroke.

A copy of the text is pasted in front, covering the original text, and given a 30% black fill. An irregular shape is then drawn over the lower portion of the text, with a fill and stroke of None.

Both lines of text and the shape are selected and grouped. The Make Mask command is applied from the Edit menu.

To complete the reverse, a rectangle is placed behind the other elements, with a fill of 100% black.

Creating distressed type

TEXT

A rubbing of embossed type, photocopied, scanned, and adjusted in Photoshop for high contrast.

PostScript type imported to Photoshop for manipulation.

Diffuse and Blur filters are applied to "deconstruct" the type.

For a different effect, the Add Noise, Diffuse, and Blur filters are applied to give the text a perforated look.

Hybrid technique

Do a rubbing of dimensional type or send type through a photocopier multiple times, then scan and rework it in Photoshop or Streamline.

Some all-digital techniques

Create an original 72-point type file in a PostScript draw program, for typographic options and control. Fill the type with black. Then import the type into Photoshop at 100 dpi, using the File Open command, with anti-aliasing on. Adjust canvas size to leave room all around the type.

View the type in an alpha channel, and make a duplicate channel to work in. Apply the Diffuse filter, set to Normal, three times (press command / F); then apply the Blur filter three times, for a "hand-inked" look. Adjust levels to increase contrast and clean up edges.

For a different look, take the same original alpha channel used above and make a new work channel. Select the type by using the Magic Wand tool on the background, and then inverting the selection. Apply the Add Noise filter; then deselect and apply the Diffuse filter, set to Normal, four times and then to Darken, three times. Finally, apply the Blur filter three times and adjust levels.

To save your finished type, choose Split Channels from the channel palette menu, and save the new files.

To export the distressed type as an outlined EPS, duplicate the type as a selection, convert the selection to PostScript paths. Set Path Tolerance in the general Preferences box for a tight (low setting) or loose (high setting) fit. Export the paths in Illustrator format. Or, save the type as a TIFF file and trace in Streamline, and save as an EPS.

The above effects can also be applied to graphic images, such as draw-program files. You can experiment and add your own touches and filter settings at each step. You may want to note what you do as you go along, so you can re-create it later.

A simple "embossed" type effect

This technique works best with bold headline or display type; it can be done in either a page layout or draw program. Tints of color can be substituted for black (see page 81, fig. 6).

1. In a page layout program, make a background area with a tint, in this case 20% black.

4. Duplicate again, fitting this copy over and centered between the previous layers. Tint this layer 20%, the same as the background. The darker layers give an illusion of shadow.

2. Create a line of type in front of the background. Give it a tint; say, 40% black.

5. For a different effect, color the layer created in step 3 white instead of a tint, giving the suggestion of highlights.

3. Duplicate the type, placing the copy on top and slightly offset; give it a 30% tint.

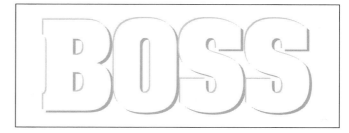

If your "embossed" type is set against a white background, color the top layer white and use lighter tints in the shadows for a subtle effect.

How to fill type with a photo image

The effect shown here is actually a combination of two effects, both involving the creation of masks for text and photo. Both effects may be accomplished in several programs; Illustrator and Quark XPress were used in this example (see page 82, fig.1).

Measure the photo image to be masked, to establish the type mask dimensions. In this case, each mask will be the full width and half the height of the photo.

For the top portion, set type in a draw program, size it to fit the layout, and fill it with white. Save it as an EPS, import it to the page layout, and place it over the photo to create a reverse.

For the bottom half, create a second draw program text file. Draw a rectangle over the text, sized to the layout, to serve as a mask. Fill text and rectangle with white, group them, and convert them to compound paths.

Working digitally with hand-drawn letterforms

If you have a piece of calligraphic art you wish to manipulate electronically or convert to a digital file, you need to start with a scan. Start with as large an original as possible, and scan it at a fairly high resolution (at least 600 ppi). Before you scan, evaluate the letterforms. If they are composed of heavy, solid strokes intended for smooth outlines, you might simply scan the original as line art and alter the image in a draw program. If the forms and their edges are more delicate, as with dry-brushed art, you may want to scan in grayscale mode and work with the image in an image-editing program, more suitable for a traditional "wet medium" feel. You can still convert it to a bitmap (line art), but will retain more control when adjusting contrast in grayscale mode (see page 82, fig.4).

Save a copy of the TIFF scan file for later use as a model or template.

A command like Streamline's Smooth Path option lets you fine-tune the lettering's edge texture by removing control points.

In the case of a set of solid-outline characters, trace your scan in Streamline, or directly in a draw program. Use the program's options to simplify the outlines by removing control points.

Bring the new vector-based art into a draw

program. You may also want to import the original scan file for reference. To clean up the letterforms' edges, begin by removing more control points, moving and tweaking others, until your lines and curves have the unwanted "bumps" ironed out of them.

If you want guidelines to refer to for matching slants, draw a straight line at the angle you want, long enough to cover the full height of the characters. Colorize the line to stand out against both background and letterforms. Then select and Option/Drag the line to duplicate it in the positions you want.

You can make adjustments in the vertical and horizontal dimensions of the shapes by selecting them and resizing in a single dimension, either manually or using a dialog box. Likewise, you can affect angles selectively or globally by using a Shear (angle) tool. You may also want to experiment with different filters. Duplicate and move copies off to the side as you work, so you can return to the steps you have made.

You may want to place an existing type character from a font into your work, for reference or inclusion in the letterforms you are creating.

You can create an entire type family based on your calligraphic forms. Fonts can be created from logos and graphics as well as letterforms. Fontographer will help you here. A digitizing tablet is a very useful tool for the electronic calligrapher.

Place a set of nonprinting guidelines to help you to position and slant characters.

Filters and commands may be used for fine adjustments to slant, thickness, and other character attributes (here, Illustrator's Shear tool was used).

Special Characters & Measurements

Macintosh special character keystrokes

©	Option / g (superscript)
®	Option / r (superscript)
™	Option / 2 (superscript)
…	Option / ;
—	Option / Shift / - (em dash)
–	Option / - (en dash)
-	- (hyphen)
"	Option / [
"	Option / Shift / [
'	Option /]
'	Option / Shift /]
" "	Smart Quotes: select as an option in Preferences
"	Option / Shift / g
´	Option / Shift / e
"	Option / , [comma] (Symbol)
'	Option / 4 (Symbol)
•	Option / 8 (Any Font)
○	Option / 8 (outline)
°	Option / Shift / 8
·	Option / Shift / 9
à	Option / `, then Character (a, e, i, o, u)
á	Option / e, then Character (a, e, i, o, u)
ä	Option / u, then Character (a, e, i, o, u)
å	Option / a Character (a, e, i, o, u)

ñ	Option / n, then 'n' Character
ç	Option / c Character
î	Option / i, then Character (a, e, i, o, u)
Ô	Shift / Option / j
¡	Option / 1
^	Option / Shift / i
~	Option / Shift / n
ˇ	Option / Shift / t
¨	Option / Shift / u
˘	Option / Shift / .
¿	Option / Shift / (/)
£	Option / 3
¢	Option / 4
∞	Option / 5
§	Option / 6
¶	Option / 7
ª	Option / 9
/	Option / Shift / 1
¤	Option / Shift / 2
‹	Option / Shift / 3
›	Option / Shift / 4
fi	Option / Shift / 5
fl	Option / Shift / 6
œ	Option / q
Œ	Option / Shift / q
æ	Option / ´

Æ	Option / Shift / ´
‡	Option / Shift / 7
†	Option / t
÷	Option / (/)
√	Option / v
≤	Option / ,
≥	Option / .
⌘	Control / q (Chicago)
	Control / t (Chicago)
■	n (Zapf Dingbats)
□	n (Zapf Dingbats / outline)
◆	u (Zapf Dingbats)
◇	u (Zapf Dingbats / outline)
❖	v (Zapf Dingbats)
⌐	Option / o (Symbol)
♥	Option / g (Symbol)
♦	Option / r (Symbol)
♣	Option / s (Symbol)
♠	Option / 2 (Symbol)
↔	Option / é (Symbol)
↑	Option / = (Symbol)
→	Shift / Option / ' (Symbol)
←	Shift / Option / u (Symbol)
↓	Shift / Option / o (Symbol)
±	Shift / Option / = (Symbol)
⊗	Option / o (Symbol)

Tack this chart up in your work area and spare yourself plenty of "look-up" time. If you find yourself using a certain group of characters or symbols frequently, make a similar chart in your favorite word processor and print it large enough to read at a distance. You may want to use this as the basis for a style sheet to import into documents.

Key combinations to obtain special characters

To create a special character in a different font, type the key combinations needed, select the character, and select the new font. If you have a lot of recurring instances, make a "bank" of these characters to copy and paste from.

To view a font's special characters

Select Key Caps from the menu. From the Key Caps menu, select the font you want to view. Press and hold the Option key to view one set of characters, the Shift key for another set of characters, and both Shift and Option together for a third set. You can type several characters, then copy and paste them where you want them.

PC special character keystrokes

Hold down ALT key and type numeric keystroke, including preceding 0.

©	ALT / 069	í	ALT / 0237	ª	ALT / 0170		
®	ALT / 0174	Î	ALT / 0206	⁄	ALT / 0147		
™	ALT / 0153	î	ALT / 0238	¤	ALT / 0164		
…	ALT / 0133	Ï	ALT / 0207	‹	ALT / 0160, 0139		
—	ALT / 0151	ï	ALT / 0239	›	ALT / 062, 0155		
–	ALT / 0150	Ò	ALT / 0210	œ	ALT / 0156		
-	ALT / 045	ò	ALT / 0242	Œ	ALT / 0140		
"	ALT / 047	Ó	ALT / 0211	æ	ALT / 0230		
"	ALT / 048	ó	ALT / 0243	Æ	ALT / 0198		
'	ALT / 0145	Ô	ALT / 0212	‡	ALT / 0135		
'	ALT / 0146	ô	ALT / 0244	†	ALT / 0134		
"	ALT / 034	Õ	ALT / 0213	÷	ALT / 0247		
´	ALT / 039	õ	ALT / 0245	√	ALT / 0214 (Symbol Proportional)		
•	ALT / 0149	Ö	ALT / 0214	≤	ALT / 0163 (Symbol Proportional)		
°	ALT / 0176	ö	ALT / 0246	≥	ALT / 0179 (Symbol Proportional)		
À	ALT / 0192	Ù	ALT / 0217		ALT / 0240 (Symbol Proportional)		
à	ALT / 0224	ù	ALT / 0249	■	ALT / 043 (Common Bullets)		
Á	ALT / 0193	Ú	ALT / 0218	□	ALT / 0108 (Common Bullets)		
á	ALT / 0225	ú	ALT / 0250	◆	ALT / 056 (Common Bullets)		
Ä	ALT / 0196	Û	ALT / 0219	◇	ALT / 057 (Common Bullets)		
ä	ALT / 0228	û	ALT / 0251	↵	ALT / 0191 (Symbol Proportional)		
Å	ALT / 0197	Ü	ALT / 0220	♥	ALT / 0169 (Symbol Proportional)		
å	ALT / 0229	ü	ALT / 0252	♦	ALT / 0168 (Symbol Proportional)		
Â	ALT / 0194	Ñ	ALT / 0209	♣	ALT / 0167 (Symbol Proportional)		
â	ALT / 0226	ñ	ALT / 0241	♠	ALT / 0170 (Symbol Proportional)		
È	ALT / 0200	ç	ALT / 0231	↔	ALT / 0171 (Symbol Proportional)		
è	ALT / 0232	¡	ALT / 0161	↑	ALT / 0173 (Symbol Proportional)		
É	ALT / 0201	^	ALT / 0136	→	ALT / 0174 (Symbol Proportional)		
é	ALT / 0233	~	ALT / 0126	←	ALT / 0172 (Symbol Proportional)		
Ê	ALT / 0202	¨	ALT / 0168	↓	ALT / 0175 (Symbol Proportional)		
ê	ALT / 0234	¿	ALT / 0191	±	ALT / 0177 (Symbol Proportional)		
Ë	ALT / 0203	£	ALT / 0163	⊗	ALT / 0196 (Symbol Proportional)		
ë	ALT / 0235	¢	ALT / 0162				
Ì	ALT / 0204	∞	ALT / 0165 (Symbol Proportional)				
ì	ALT / 0236	§	ALT / 0167				
Í	ALT / 0205	¶	ALT / 0182				

Zapf Dingbats

Macintosh keystrokes

Keyboard Character	Zapf Dingbat Keystroke	Option / Keystroke	Option /Shift / Keystroke	Shift / Keystroke
1	☞	②	↗	✂
2	☛	♥	→	✠
3	✓	❣	➔	✁
4	✔	❥	→	✄
5	✗	⑤	→	☎
6	✘	❤	⇛	✿
7	✗	❧	⇛	✆
8	✘	❦	ℊ	☞
9	✚	❻	➡	✈
0	✎	❼	➢	✉
-	✍	❼	❽	✽
=	†	②	⑥	☞
q	❑	❻	❺	✱
w	◗	❷	➣	✳
e	❄	♠	♠	✛
r	❐	♣	➤	✻
t	▼			✴
y	❙	⑨	▸	✹
u	◆	①	①	✺
i	❄	➹	➹	☆
o	❏	❿	④	✩
p	❒	❹	❸	✫
[	✼	❾	❿	❛
]	✼	→	→	❝
\	✼	⑧	⑨	❞
a	❀	{	☽	✡
s	▲	❧	⇨	✶
d	❆	❶	⇨	✤
f	❅	⑤	⇨	◆
g	✳	◆	➟	✧
h	✸	➜	⇨	★
j	✲	⑦	⇨	✪
k	✱	☛	⑧	☆
l	●	③	⇨	✬
;	✜	⑩	⊃	✚
'	⌖	⑨	③	✂
z	▮	❽	➜	✵
x	❘	⑥	⇒	✴
c	✻	}	(	✛
v	❖	④	↕	✺
b	✿	❺	➝	✛
n	◼	➴	➴	☆
m	◯	⑩	➡	★
,	✌	⑦	➵	✛
.	✎	⑧	➶	✝
/	✐	↔	①	✞

Option / Space	❶
Option / `, then Shift/ a	❷
Option / n, then Shift/ a	❸
Option / n, then Shift/ o	❹

PC keystrokes

Symbol	Code	Symbol	Code
☞	ALT / 049	✛	ALT / 060
☛	ALT / 050	⊕	ALT / 039
✓	ALT / 051	▮	ALT / 0122
✔	ALT / 052	❘	ALT / 0120
✗	ALT / 053	✳	ALT / 096
✘	ALT / 054	❖	ALT / 0118
✗	ALT / 055	✸	ALT / 098
✘	ALT / 056	◼	ALT / 0110
✚	ALT / 057	◗	ALT / 0109
✎	ALT / 048	✌	ALT / 044
✍	ALT / 045	✏	ALT / 046
†	ALT / 061	✎	ALT / 047
❑	ALT / 0111	②	ALT / 0193
◗	ALT / 0119	♥	ALT / 0170
✳	ALT / 0101	❣	ALT / 0163
❐	ALT / 0112	❥	ALT / 0162
▼	ALT / 0116	⑤	ALT / 0176
❙	ALT / 0121	❤	ALT / 0164
◆	ALT / 0117	❧	ALT / 0166
❄	ALT / 0100	❦	ALT / 0165
❏	ALT / 0113	❻	ALT / 0187
❒	ALT / 0114	❼	ALT / 0188
✼	ALT / 099	❼	ALT / 0208
✼	ALT / 0105	②	ALT / 0173
❀	ALT / 097	❧	ALT / 0167
▲	ALT / 0115	❶	ALT / 0182
❆	ALT / 0102	⑤	ALT / 0196
❅	ALT / 0192	◆	ALT / 0169
✳	ALT / 0103	➜	ALT / 0250
✸	ALT / 0104	⑦	ALT / 0198
✲	ALT / 0106	☛	ALT / 0251
✱	ALT / 0107	③	ALT / 0194
●	ALT / 0108	⑩	ALT / 0201

Decimal equivalents for fractions of an inch

Symbol	Code		Symbol	Code
❾	ALT / 0190		⇔	ALT / 0235
❽	ALT / 0189		⇖	ALT / 0236
⑥	ALT / 0197		➡	ALT / 0253
④	ALT / 0195		⇨	ALT / 0238
❺	ALT / 0186		⇨	ALT / 0239
↘	ALT / 0244		⇨	ALT / 0241
⑩	ALT / 0180		⊃	ALT / 0242
⑦	ALT / 0178		➡	ALT / 0252
⑧	ALT / 0179		⇛	ALT / 0254
↔	ALT / 0214		↕	ALT / 0215
↗	ALT / 0218		➞	ALT / 0245
→	ALT / 0219		↘	ALT / 0247
→	ALT / 0220		➡	ALT / 0229
→	ALT / 0213		➡	ALT / 0243
→	ALT / 0217		➷	ALT / 0249
➡	ALT / 0223		①	ALT / 0192
➡	ALT / 0224		✂	ALT / 033
✶	ALT / 0161		✠	ALT / 064
➡	ALT / 0225		✂	ALT / 035
➢	ALT / 0226		✄	ALT / 036
❽	ALT / 0209		☎	ALT / 037
⑥	ALT / 0177		❀	ALT / 094
❺	ALT / 0206		✆	ALT / 038
➢	ALT / 0227		☜	ALT / 042
♠	ALT / 0171		✈	ALT / 040
➤	ALT / 0228		✉	ALT / 041
▶	ALT / 0231		✿	ALT / 095
①	ALT / 0172		☞	ALT / 043
↗	ALT / 0246		✴	ALT / 081
④	ALT / 0175		☆	ALT / 080
❸	ALT / 0204		✡	ALT / 065
⑩	ALT / 0211		☆	ALT / 075
⑨	ALT / 0200		★	ALT / 079
➤	ALT / 0248		✪	ALT / 074
⇨	ALT / 0234			

3rds

1/3	.333
2/3	.666

4ths

1/4"	.25
3/4"	.75
2/4"	.5
1/2"	.5

8ths

1/8"	.125
2/8"	.25
3/8	.375
4/8	.5
5/8	.625
6/8	.75
7/8	.875

16ths

1/16	.062
3/16	.187
5/16	.312
7/16	.437
9/16	.562
11/16	.687
13/16	.812
15/16	.937

32nds

1/32	.031
3/32	.093
5/32	.156
7/32	.218
9/32	.281
11/32	.343
13/32	.406
15/32	.486
17/32	.531
19/32	.593
21/32	.656
23/32	.718
25/32	.781
27/32	.843
29/32	.906
31/32	.968

64ths

1/64	.015
3/64	.046
5/64	.078
7/64	.109
9/64	.140
11/64	.171
13/64	.203
15/64	.234
17/64	.265
19/64	.296
21/64	.328
23/64	.359
25/64	.390
27/64	.421
29/64	.453
31/64	.484
33/64	.515
35/64	.546
37/64	.578
39/64	.609
41/64	.640
43/64	.671
45/64	.703
47/64	.734
49/64	.765
51/64	.796
53/64	.828
55/64	.859
57/64	.890
59/64	.921
61/64	.953
63/64	.984

Unit conversion table

Points =	Picas =	Millimeters =	Inches
0.25 pt		0.09 mm	0.004″
0.05 pt		0.18 mm	0.007″
1 pt	0.08 picas	0.35 mm	0.014″
1.5 pt		0.53 mm	0.021″
2 pt	0.17 picas	0.71 mm	0.028″
2.83 pt		1.00 mm	0.039″
3 pt	0.25 picas	1.06 mm	0.042″
4 pt	0.33 picas	1.41 mm	0.056″
5 pt	0.42 picas		
6 pt	0.50 picas	2.12 mm	0.083″
7 pts	0.58 picas		
8 pt	0.67 picas	2.82 mm	0.111″
9 pt	0.75 picas		
10 pt	0.85 picas		
11 pt	0.92 picas		
12 pt	1.00 pica	4.23 mm	0.167″
2 picas		8.47 mm	0.333″
3 picas		12.7 mm	0.5″
4 picas		16.93 mm	0.667″
6 picas		25.40 mm	1″
8 picas		33.87 mm	1.333″
12 picas		50.80 mm	2″
24 picas		101.60 mm	4″
48 picas		203.20 mm	8″
52 picas		215.90 mm	8.5″
66 picas		279.40 mm	11″
102 picas		431.80 mm	17″

Universal QuicKeys

Macintosh

Command	Keystrokes
Cancel	Command / Period (.) or Esc.
Close	Command / W
Copy	Command / C
Cut	Command / X
New (folder or file)	Command / N
Open	Command / O
Paste	Command / V
Print	Command / P
Quit	Command / Q
Save	Command / S
Select All	Command / A
Undo	Command / Z

PC

Command	Keystrokes *
Cancel	Control / ALT / Delete
Close	Control / ALT / W
Copy	Control / ALT / C
Cut	Control / ALT / X
New (folder or file)	Control / ALT / N
Open	Control / ALT / O
Paste	Control / ALT / V
Print	Control / ALT / P
Quit (Exit)	Control / Q
Save	Control / ALT / S
Select All	Control / ALT / A
Undo	Control / ALT / Z

* Verify for individual software

Tricks & Special Effects
How to draw polygons and stars

This technique works in most drawing or page layout applications; only the names of commands and some of the tools change. Some draw programs have special tools and filters for creating these figures. To ensure accuracy, use guidelines and activate the Snap to Guides option.

Polygon

Determine how many sides your polygon will have. Divide 360 by the number of sides.
In this case, we'll make a decagon (10 sides).
$360° ÷ 10 = 36°.$

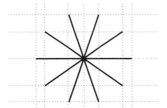 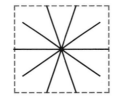

1. Establish a center point with two guides intersecting at 90°. Draw a vertical line with a Line tool and rotate at 36°. Duplicate the line five times, rotating each at 36° from the last (at 72°, 108°, 144°, and 180° respectively).

2. Group and lock the lines. This produces five diameters with 10 equally-spaced endpoints.

3. Use a Line or Polygon tool to connect the endpoints around the polygon's perimeter.

4. Delete the radiating lines.

Another approach: draw radii that fan out from the center point—this works best for polygons with odd numbers of sides.

Star

Begin a star in the same manner as the polygon, by radiating lines in a circle. You'll need twice as many radii as points in the star (10 lines for a 5-pointed star).

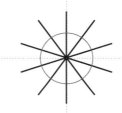 

1. Draw a circle to locate the inner points of the star, centered over the center point of the lines.

2. Using a Line or Polygon tool, draw a continuous line around the star's perimeter, connecting endpoints with points where the circle intersects the radii.

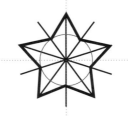 

3. Give the completed outline the stroke width you want.

4. Delete the inner circle and radiating lines.

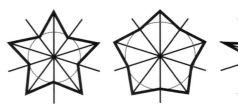

The size of the inner circle determines the star's shape, making it "fat" to "spiky."

How to create stroked type effects

The Outline type-style command produces weak outlines, bad letterspacing, and few editing options.

Using the Outline type-style command in your page layout or word-processing program will produce amateurish results, and may not output at all on an imagesetter. The correct way to create outlined type is in a draw or image-editing program. This not only produces better results, but also offers many more choices of effects. Here are a few, all based on the same line of normal type:

To the right is the same type, set in a draw program and given a white fill and stroke values of .25 point, .5 point, and 1 point respectively, then kerned.

To achieve the effect of a thicker stroke, duplicate the type, stack the copies, and give the background copy a thick stroke (6 points here) and the top copy no stroke and a white fill.

This layering will prevent the strokes from spreading into the body of the type, as it does here.

The same effect, but with the strokes set to rounded "Join" attributes.

To produce the above effects the type was set in a draw program, kerned as required, and then converted to outlines (or paths), as shown above. It is a good idea to save an unconverted backup version of the file for later editing; type converted to outlines is no longer "type."

For this soft-edge effect, the type (1) is given a 6-point-stroke (2), converted to Outlines, and imported into an image-editing program, where a Gaussian Blur filter is applied; in this case, a 9-pixel radius was used (3). This is saved as a TIFF file. A white-filled, unstroked EPS version of the type is then superimposed over the blured image (4).

How to make type swirl

OVER HILL, OVER DALE

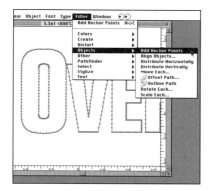

1. Set your line of type in a draw program and convert it to outlines.

2. With the type selected, add anchor points (in Illustrator, choose Filter/Objects /Add Anchor Points). You may need to repeat the process a few times with simpler typefaces like this sans serif.

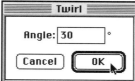

3. Select Filter/Distort/Twirl and enter the desired angle. In this case, 30° was used.

You can now add outline, fills, and other effects. Here, the type was copied, filled, and stroked, and superimposed over the original type.

How to fit display type to a shape

WORLDVIEW PRODUCTIONS WORLDVIEW PRODUCTIONS

1. Set your display type in a draw program, center it and convert it to outlines. Group each line of type.

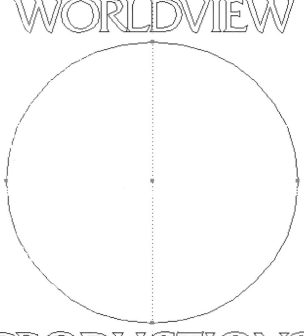

2. Draw the shape that the text will fit around. In this case. we want the edges closest to the circle to hug its outline, and the opposing edges to remain horizontal. Work in Artwork view, so you can see all paths as you select and alter them. Arrange the type in relation to the shape and its center reference line.

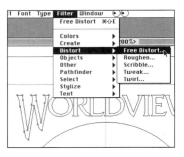

3. Select the bottom half of the letters above the shape and left of the center line and choose Filters/Distort/Free Distort. Pull the Distort control points in the direction of the shape and click OK.

4. Adjust and reapply the Distort filter, repeating the process on both sides until the text wraps as you want it to. Tweak individual control points for a more exact fit.

5. Save the final result as an EPS, adding the image around which the type is to wrap (see page 83, fig.4).

How to make a curved gradient fill

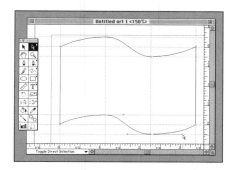

1. In a draw program, create the curved shape to be filled with a graduated blend.

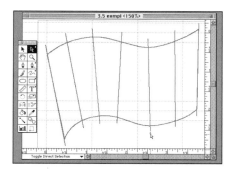

2. Draw straight guide lines at right angles to the curves. Stroke these lines with the colors you want to include in the gradated fill.

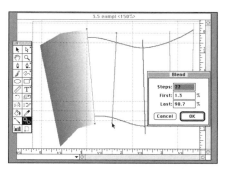

3. Select the first two lines, choose the blend tool, and select end points on both the first and second lines.

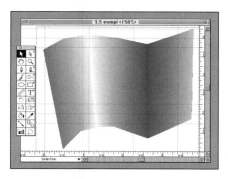

4. Repeat until you have created a fill the length of the original shape.

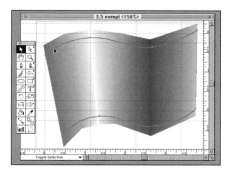

5. Move the original curved shape to the front.

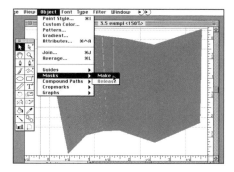

6. Select all and choose Make Masks from the Object menu.

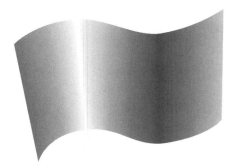

7. The completed series of blends (see page 82, fig. 2).

How to create a vignette effect with type

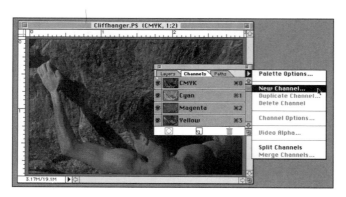

1. Open an image file in an image-editing application and create a new channel.

2. In the new channel, import or type the text you want to vignette and scale it to fit.

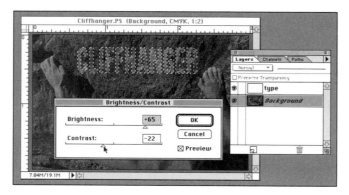

3. Return to the image channel and choose Load Selection. Adjust brightness and contrast to achieve the effect you want.

4. The final effect (see page 82, fig. 3).

How to create an icon

To dress up the Mac files you create and distribute, you can make custom icons to replace the default icons that symbolize files on the desktop. This is a great way to identify graphic files that are not equipped with a PICT resource file for menu selection.

Be sure to turn off File Sharing before editing the icon of a disk containing a shared file.

To modify an existing icon

Select a file, folder, or disk. Choose Get Info (Command/I) from the File menu, and click on the icon in the window to select it. Copy the icon (Command/C), open a new document in a paint or image-editing program, and paste the copied icon.

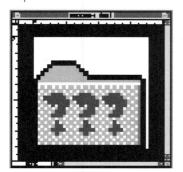

After you have modified the icon to your satisfaction, select it and copy it. Return to the Get Info window, click on the icon, and paste. Close the window; now your file has a unique icon.

To design an icon from scratch

Create an image in any paint or image-editing program, sized to 32 x 32 pixels or less, at 72 dpi. Keep the images very simple.

Select the new image, copy, and paste in the Get Info window.

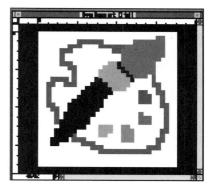

You can create an icon for any file except the Trash Can. You can also copy and paste icons between files, and re-icon your drives and disks.

To return the "Info Box" icon to its original state, select it and use the Cut command.

How to create a screen capture

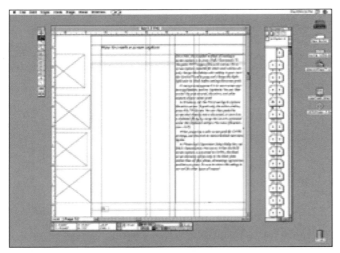

Shift/Command/3 captures the entire Mac screen image, which can then be modified in an image-editing program.

On a Mac, the simplest method of creating a screen capture is to press Shift/Command/3. You get a TIFF image of the entire screen.

In Windows, hit the PrtScreen key to capture the entire screen. To grab only the active window, press Alt/PrtScreen. You can then paste the screen shot directly into a document, or save it as a clipboard file by using the Save As command under the Clipboard utility's File menu (file extension: .CLP). This process may require a special utility in some Windows systems.

When preparing a color screen grab for CMYK printing, use the technique below to make the black text more legible.

For a screen capture intended for black-and-white output, change the desktop color setting in your monitor control panel to grays and change the highlight color to black before making the screen grab.

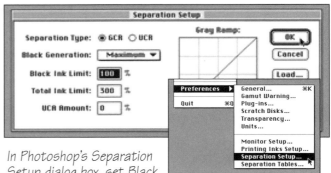

In Photoshop's Separation Setup dialog box, set Black Generation to Maximum. When the RGB screen capture is converted to CMYK, the black screen elements will go only to the black plate rather than all four plates, eliminating registration problems on press. Be sure to return the setting to normal for other types of images!

A more precise approach is to use a screen capture application, such as Captivate. You can then control the area covered, the colors, and other aspects of your screen grab.

How to use bitmap effects in Photoshop

Effects available in Photoshop's Bitmap Mode conversion command can produce line-art effects for various graphic uses. You can also experiment with various dot shapes. Print the image out before you save, to see if you want the effect. Files saved as TIFFs in this way are very compact, and become bitmapped line art.

These effects are especially useful when converting continuous-tone art for use in process silk-screen printing.

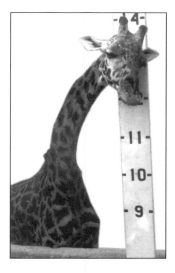

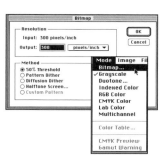

To create effects, first size the original image to its intended reproduction size. Then choose one of the bitmap modes and convert the image.

Some images may benefit from posterization before mode conversion, as with this posterized (8 gray levels) and diffusion-dithered photo.

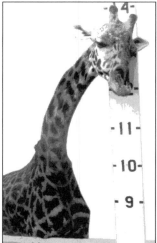

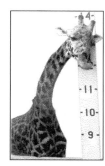

Diffusion dither   Pattern dither

The Diffusion Dithering option produces a random dot effect that simulates stippled pen-and-ink in a single-color image, or stochastic printing patterns in a multicolor image. For a single-color image, convert it to a bitmap using the Diffusion Dither setting and save as a TIFF file.

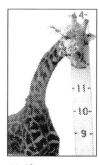

Halftone screen   Halftone screen
(150 lpi, ellipse)   (80 lpi, cross)

Try combining different line screen resolutions with various dot shapes in the halftone option. Results will depend in part upon the final output resolution.

For four-color-process use, convert the image to CMYK and save it as an EPS file, using the DCS option. Throw out the resulting preview file, saving files of the four channels with C, M, Y, and K respectively appended to the file names. Then open each file and use the Adjust Levels command to set the Output Levels at 15, removing all pure black tones. Finally, use the Bitmap Mode command with the Diffusion Dither option, setting resolution at 100 ppi. Save as TIFF files. Output each file separately, with crop and registration marks.

Bitmap effects

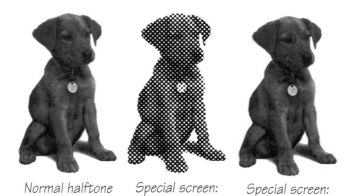

Normal halftone

Special screen: 30 lpi, 45°, line

Special screen: 60 lpi, 60°, square

Picture Screening Specifications

Halftone

Screen: 30 (lpi) Angle: 45°

Pattern

○ Dot ● Line ○ Ellipse ○ Square
○ Ordered Dither

☐ Display Halftoning [OK] [Cancel]

Halftones generated with Quark's Other Screen option, found under the Style menu. Print out the screened image to make sure it is the effect you want, and to serve as a guide when the page is output from an image processor.

Halftone Screen

Halftone Screen

Frequency: 150 lines/inch ▼

Angle: 45 degrees

Shape: Round ▼

[OK] [Cancel]

When you convert a grayscale image to a halftone using Photoshop's screen option, you get a black-and-white line-art file (the white areas are actually transparent) (see page 83, fig.1).

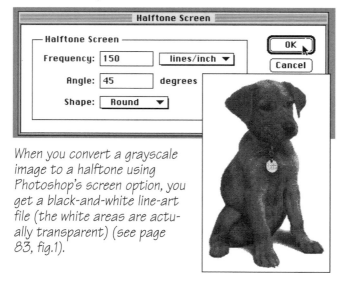

Custom screens

Custom screens can turn a conventional photo into an interesting graphic. You can experiment with this effect in various programs: In Quark XPress, choose Other Screen; in Pagemaker, use Image Control; in Freehand, use the Halftone palette.

Try screen rulings between 20 and 60 lpi, experimenting with different angles and screen types. If you are sending the file to a PostScript imagesetter, be sure to standardize your settings for the page and let the operator know that the page needs to be output with those settings; otherwise, the imagesetter's software may override them.

To retain more control over grayscale image output, bypass PostScript entirely and convert the images to bitmaps, using the Halftone Screen in Photoshop.

Images created in this way are transparent in their "white" areas, allowing some interesting overlay effects. Or you can superimpose an EPS image with a clipping path over a bitmapped TIFF.

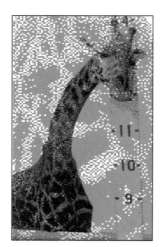

TIFF halftones, superimposed

EPS with clipping path, placed over a TIFF

A coarse bitmap screen effect
You can use this effect in a variety of ways.

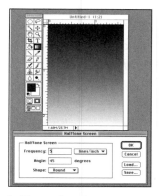 

In Photoshop, begin a grayscale file. Create a gradient from top to bottom. Convert it to a bitmap, using Halftone Screen, with Frequency set to 5; use a round shape.

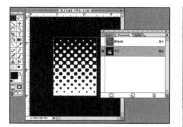 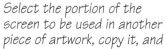

Select the portion of the screen to be used in another piece of artwork, copy it, and paste it into a new channel in the artwork file. Load the channel and adjust hues, saturations, and levels, or experiment with filters to create various effects (see page 83, fig. 3).

 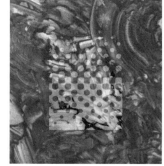

Save an image as a bitmap TIFF at 1,200 ppi, with a round halftone dot, a frequency of 60, and an angle of 45°. Trace it in Streamline and convert it to open outlines, using a noise suppression of 8 pixels and a tolerance of 2.1.

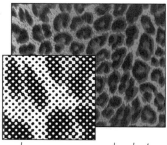

You can then open the art in a draw program and colorize it, use it as a mask, or apply other effects. This technique works with any image containing good contrast.

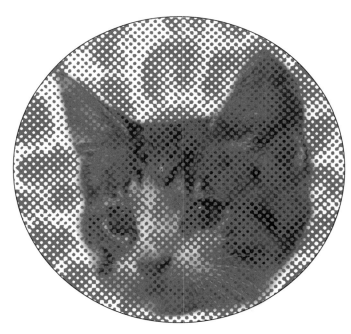

Creating a simple bitmap texture

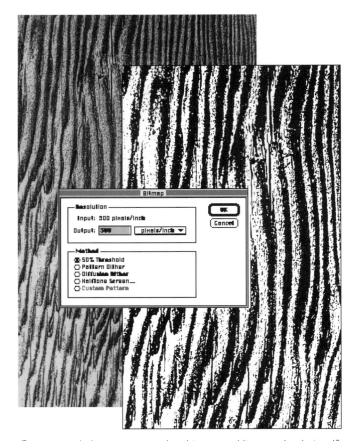

Here is a quick way to make an interesting framing device for text or pictures, or a page background.

Choose a high-contrast black-and-white texture (photocopied photos work well). Scan as a grayscale image. Adjust contrast until the midtones have separated into black or white. Convert to a bitmap image with a 50% threshold, and save as a TIFF.

Import the image into a page layout program; colorize and shade it. Colorize the background of the picture box. For a different effect, stack several duplicate boxes, altering the image slightly in each. Colorize the background of only the bottommost box.

An alternate method: scan the real thing (textured fabric, a piece of bark, a marble tile sample, gravel) sandwiched between two clear surfaces.

The scanned photo, converted to bitmapped line art, lends itself to limitless graphic treatments with variations in color, shading, and juxtaposition of stacked copies (see page 82, fig. 5).

Place loose materials between two sheets of glass or plastic, taped together. Scan as grayscale, then convert to a high-contrast bitmap.

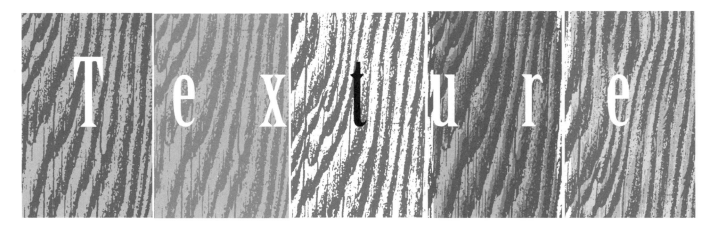

How to prepare multitoned images for print

Screens for duotone, tritone, or quadtone images must be set to different values, so that the different inks do not directly overprint each other (see page 83, figs. 5 and 6).

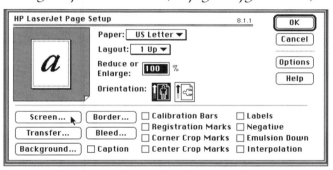

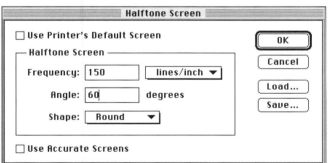

When importing the image to Pagemaker, screen values should be set in Photoshop before saving the file as EPS, as shown above. Choose Page Setup and click on the Screen button. Enter screen values for each ink (90° apart for a duotone; check with your printer) and save as an EPS. Be sure to check the "Include Halftone Screen" box.

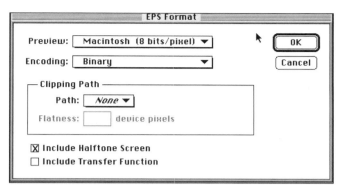

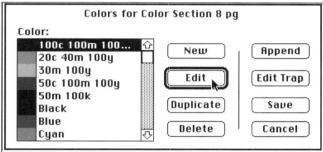

When importing the image to QuarkXPress, save the EPS file without screen values. Then, in Quark, open the Edit Color dialog box, select each color used in the EPS image, and choose Edit. In the Screen Values pop-up list, assign values other than Process Black to the inks.

Be sure to keep color names consistent in all applications (don't use the name PMS 200 in Photoshop and Logo Red in Quark).

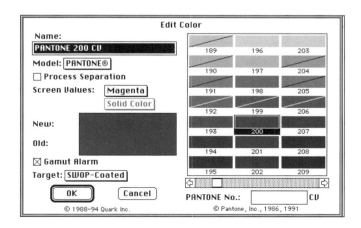

Colorizing line art

To colorize line art in Photoshop

Scan the line art at 300 dpi in grayscale setting, increasing the contrast for crisp lines. Convert the image to RGB mode. Select the art in the Background layer and float it (Command / J). Create a new layer named "art" for the floating selection. Go back to the background; layer and clear it (Delete). Make a new layer called "color" between the other two. Activate the "art" layer, select an area with the Magic Wand tool, with the Layers palette in Multiply mode. Switch to the "color" layer, choose a fill color, and fill the selection (Option/Delete). If you wish, you can then use other tools and filters to add effects to colorized selections.

To colorize a scanned image in Illustrator (earlier versions than 6.0), you first need to save it as a TIFF and trace it in Streamline.

TIFF images can be colorized directly in Freehand.

There is software on the market specifically for colorizing black-and-white line art; if you expect to do a lot of this, shop around.

Line art, scanned in grayscale setting, is brought into Photoshop…

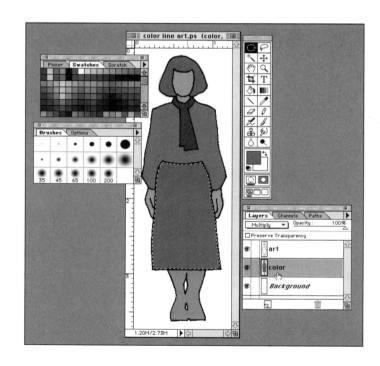

…and given its own layer. A color layer is created and colors are added to selected sections.

Finally, effects are added to the color layer. Here, the Airbrush tool was used to apply shading (see page 84, fig. 1).

How to convert a color image to line art

1. Scan the image with slightly increased contrast and bring into Photoshop; convert to grayscale.

2. Crop the image as desired and adjust contrast again.

3. Open a new grayscale file with the same dimensions as the original. Returning to the original, activate the Channels palette. Increase the contrast to produce a version mostly filled in with black.

4. Copy the black channel to the other file. Repeat this step several times, reverting the original to normal contrast, then lightening and increasing contrast a bit more each time.

5. You will end up with a file containing versions of the original in various degrees of high contrast; the composite of these will be a posterized image.

This works well for creating images destined for silk-screen printing, especially logos (see page 84, fig. 2).

How to make drop shadows in Photoshop

Transparent drop shadow

1. Open a file in Photoshop at 250 ppi, slightly larger than the object casting the shadow. In the Layers palette, select New, change the mode to Background, and click OK.

2. Select the layer in the Layers palette, then select Blur/Gaussian Blur in the Filters menu. Choose a setting between 4 and 8.

3. Use the opacity slider in the Layers palette to lighten the shadow, using a setting between 35% and 60%.

4. Convert to Bitmap mode, flattening layers. Select Diffusion Dither, at 1,260 ppi. Save this as an EPS file, with the Transparent Whites box checked. You can now use this shadow on top of another background in a page layout program.

Another drop shadow technique

1. Begin with a background layer, either white or a tint or texture. Bring the object you want to shadow into the file, isolated on its own layer. You may need to remove any extra image surrounding the object on its layer; the layer should be transparent except for the object itself.

2. Duplicate the object's layer by dragging it onto the New Layer icon, then sandwich the new layer between object and background layers. In the new layer, choose Fill from the Edit menu. Set the contents menu to Black, with 100% opacity, and click on the Preserve Transparency option to fill only the object's outline with black. Next, choose Gaussian Blur from the Filter menu and adjust the blur radius setting to your preference (try 4 pixels). Offset the shadow with the Move tool or adjust with your keyboard's arrow keys a pixel at a time. Finally, use the shadow layer's opacity slider to adjust its darkness. To save the file for export, flatten the image to one layer (see page 84, fig. 3, top).

Another method

Place EPS art into an alpha channel. Return to the main channel, choose Load Selection and Inverse. Feather the selection by specifying a value in the Feather Selection dialog box from the Select menu. Fill the selection with a percentage of black (30-50% yields the best range of grays). For best results in CMYK printing, use a 4-color gray formula, for example: 30%C, 27%M, 25%Y, 30%K (you can adjust the formula, but maintain this order and ratio). Now delete the alpha channel and save the file as a TIFF. Place this file into a page layout, below and offset from the object being shadowed.

    This technique can be used effectively with type (see page 84, fig. 3, center).

Shadow

Always make a separate, editable drop shadow file for type, rather than using the "shadow" text attribute.

Another method for type drop shadows

In a page layout program, set up a text box with font, attributes, kerning, etc., making sure the background is None. Duplicate or Step-and-Repeat the text, placing it at an offset to the original. Apply a new color and tint to the shadow text and send it behind the original. Group the two boxes for positioning (see page 84, fig. 3, center).

Shadow

How to create a drop shadow for a group of page elements

Lay out on your page the elements that will require a drop shadow. With all the elements visible on screen at 100% size, make a screen capture of them (Command/Shift/3). Open the screen capture in Photoshop and crop to the relevant area. Convert to grayscale mode for a single-color shadow, CMYK for a process tint.

    Using the Magic Wand tool, select the white areas, invert the selection (Inverse in the Select menu), and press Delete. Fill the selection with the tint desired. Deselect and apply a Gaussian Blur filter, with a range of 6 to 10 pixels. Save the shadow image as a TIFF or an EPS file and import it into your page layout, placing it behind and slightly offset from the page elements (see page 84, fig. 3, bottom).

How to create glow effects

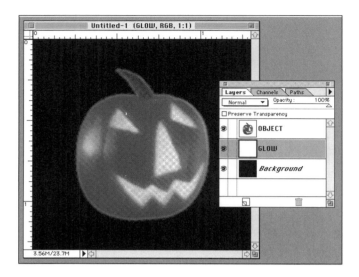

To create a glow around an object, you can use a method similar to that used for drop shadows.

Begin in Photoshop with a background layer in a relatively dark color, and an object layer. Duplicate the object layer, make a sandwich, and fill the new layer with 100% white, with Preserve Transparency chosen. Now choose Other/Minimum from the Filter menu to spread the glow's edges outward.

Experiment with the radius settings (try 6 pixels). Choose the Gaussian Blur filter to soften the glow's edge, and adjust the radius setting. The glow should be placed directly behind the object for the proper effect (see page 85, fig. 1).

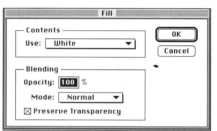

With your three layers in place, select the middle layer and fill with opaque white (or any light color), Preserve Transparency activated.

Soften the glow's edge with the Gaussian Blur filter, again adjusting radius setting for the desired effect. When used behind type, this technique produces a neon effect.

Select Other/Minimum from the Filters menu to create the glow, and expand it outward by adjusting the radius setting.

How to create a photo vignette

One way to vary the look of your pages is to soften the edges of some photos in the layout, easy to do in an image-editing program. Basically, you make a feathered selection of the part of the photo you want to retain, and remove the rest.

When you make a feathered selection, remember that the feather value designated for the selection marquee can be misleading. The actual feathered border can be several times as wide as the setting would indicate; half inside the marquee border and half outside. For example, with a setting of 10, the image will fade to white over a span of almost 50 pixels, with about 20 of these outside the marquee. This means that your selected area should be about 40 pixels smaller than the entire image in all directions in order to get a vignette all around. Use the Info palette to check your position when making the selection.

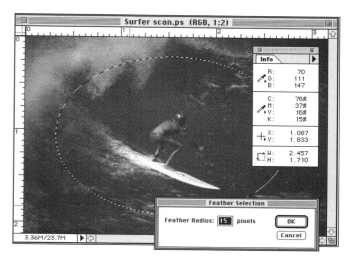

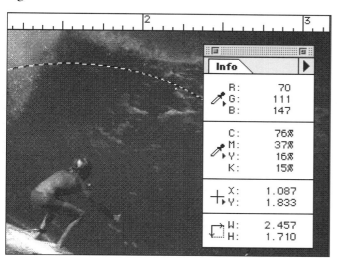

Use the Info palette to check the position of your selected area when preparing to make a vignette, keeping in mind the total number of pixels affected. In this way, you are sure to leave enough room for the edge to fade to 0 dots.

To create a vignette in Photoshop, make a feathered selection of the image area you want to show, then choose the Inverse command, selecting the portion to be removed. Delete this area, making sure that the background is set to white.

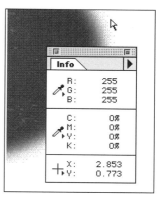

Another method: Make the feathered selection and copy it. Open a new, blank file and paste the selection into it.

You can check the edges of the vignette with an Eyedropper tool and the Info palette to be sure that the image fades to 0 where you want it to.

As with any image edit, it is a good idea to save an unedited original version of the image file (see page 85, fig. 2).

How to create interesting picture frames and edge effects

"Torn-edge" effect

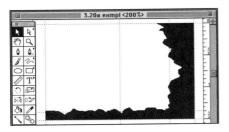

1. Create a masking shape with a "torn edge" in a draw program. Fill the shape with black, then duplicate it, placing the copy above and filling it with white.

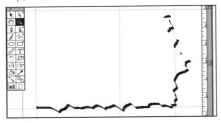

2. The copy should be slightly offset, and 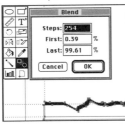 modified to cover the straight edges of the lower black shape. Select both shapes and create a blend for a soft shadow.

3. Place the mask, saved as an EPS, over a photo in a page layout program (see page 85, fig. 3, top).

An outline edge effect

1. A modification of the torn-edge mask technique produces a complex photo framing device. Create a silhouette shape in a draw program, or import a clip-art image and remove all elements within its outline.

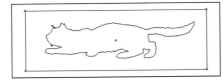

2. Draw a box greater in size than the silhouette, and centered over it.

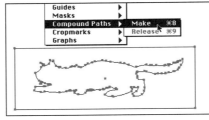

3. Select both items and choose Compound Paths. Fill the object with a background color. Place an image behind this mask, or place the mask over a photo in a page layout program (see page 83, fig. 3, center).

A softer-edged effect

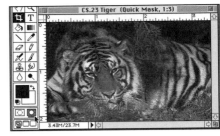

1. Open an image in Photoshop and choose Quickmask mode.

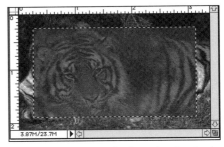

2. Select an area with the selection tool a good distance away from the image's edge. Fill it with black, deselect, and apply a Gaussian Blur (with a radius of around 10–20 pixels).

 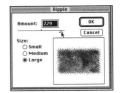

 3. Select a filter and apply its effect. Go back to Standard mode and choose Delete (see page 85, fig. 3, bottom).

Working with ghosted and split images

The ghosting technique is handy for creating a screened-back area in a photo so overprinted type can show up clearly against the background. It can be accomplished in several ways, using different types of software, depending on the type of image used and effect desired.

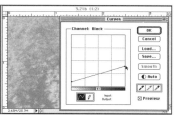

To create the effect in a page layout program, stack duplicate copies of the image over each other, in exact position, and then crop and stylize one of the copies. Single-color TIFF images work best here. In Pagemaker, simply use the Power-Paste option. In Quark, change the Step and Repeat offsets to 0, then perform the copy and paste. Then crop or mask the topmost image. To apply the ghosting effect, set the cropped photo to a tint. For greater control, adjust the curves of the image to reduce contrast, preserve highlight detail, and increase type legibility. This will allow you to easily try different settings with the type in place.

To apply ghosting to a color image or an EPS file, it is best to do the work in an image-editing program. You can create a version of the image with a flattened tonal curve and reduced saturation, then import and carefully position it over the full-toned version in the page layout. This will allow the most flexibility; you can adjust the size of the ghost area with type in place.

Or you can apply the ghosting effect to the image in the editing program, adjusting the saturation and curves down in a selected area. This requires that you use either a template or careful measurements to ghost the area in correct size and position. However, it also allows you to create a ghost with soft (feathered) edges and an irregular shape, using the Path tool (see page 85, fig. 4, top and bottom).

How to apply selective colorization to a photo

These techniques are useful for highlighting part of a photo, to draw the viewer's attention to that spot. Start with a color photo in an image-editing program, then selectively subtract color from it (see page 86, fig. 1).

1. The simplest method is most useful for uncomplicated shapes.

2. Create a path around the chosen color area with a pen tool, save the path, and make it into a selection.

3. Invert the selection, to work on the surrounding area.

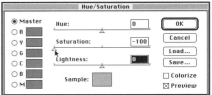

4. Desaturate the selected area, removing the color and turning that area into a grayscale image. Varying the desaturation can produce a hand-tinted effect. The final effect leaves full color in the portion of the image that is being emphasized.

1. A more painterly approach utilizes multiple layers in your image-editing software. Start with a color image file.

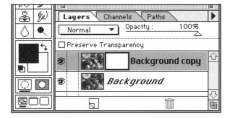

2. Position a copy of the color original on top of the original's layer and desaturate the copy to create a grayscale layer. Choose Add Layer Mask from the Layers palette menu. Make the foreground color black.

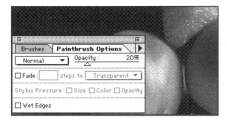

3. Select a Paintbrush or an Airbrush tool, and begin painting the areas where you want color to appear. These areas will become transparent, revealing the colors in the lower layer.

4. To return any areas to grayscale, switch the foreground color to white and paint over them again.

Isolating an area of a photo for impact

1. Open a CMYK photo image in Photoshop.

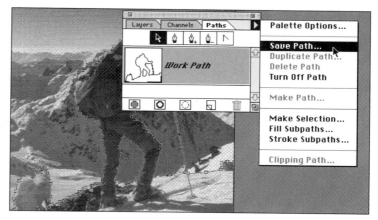

2. Using the Paths tool, draw a path around the area you wish to emphasize. Save the path. Create a second path for the background shape and save.

3. Activate the first path and choose Select/Save Selection; do the same for the second path.

4. Choose Select/Load Selection and choose channel 5.

5. Choose Select/Inverse, then choose the Gaussian Blur filter, using the setting of your choice. At this point, you can apply other effects to the background, such as desaturation.

6. Click on the CMYK channel in the Channels palette. Pressing Shift/Option, click on channel 5 and then 6. Choose Select/Inverse, and delete (see page 86, fig. 3).

How to create embossed effects with objects and text

Use Photoshop's Layers and Channels to apply a raised effect to text or a simple shape (such as a logo). It can be an effective way to subtly integrate type or graphics into a photo or textured background.

1. Open the background image to be embossed.

2. Choose the New Channel icon in the Channels palette; name the channel "Object Mask" and choose Color Indicates: Selected Areas.

3. Import or place the artwork (black-and-white line art works best) in the new channel.

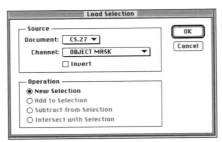

4. Select the Layers palette and create a new layer. Choose Load Selection from the Select menu, with these settings active: the current document's name; Channel: Object Mask; Invert: deselected.

5. Choose Fill from the Edit menu, using black at 100% opacity. Deselect the outline. To emboss the image, choose the Gaussian Blur filter; try about a 3-pixel radius.

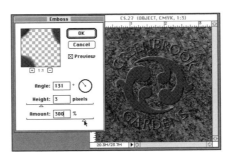

6. Choose Emboss from the Stylize filters menu. Select an angle. Height: use the same value as for the Gaussian blur. Amount: 300%.

7. Choose Hard Light from the layer's mode menu. Choose Load Selection, with these settings: Channel: Object Mask; Invert: selected. Press Delete. You can reposition the embossed shape as necessary by moving the layer around. Discard the mask channel (see page 86, fig. 2).

How to make and use a tracing template of a page layout

When creating either electronic or traditional-media artwork for a page layout, it is helpful to have a tracing template to work from. With a template, you can determine sizes and placement with precision.

To make a template from your page layout for tracing in traditional media is simple: just assign border values to key elements of the page and print it out.

To make a template for electronic use, do as you would for traditional media, but save the page as an EPS file. You can then open the file in an image-editing program and resave it, choosing different file formats for different uses:

Save as a TIFF to retrace the guidelines in Streamline, for import into the application to be used for creating the artwork. Also use this format when bringing the template into another page layout or drawing application.

Save as a PICT file for use as a tracing template in a draw program.

You can screen back or colorize the template, to differentiate it from the artwork in progress.

75

Health & Safety
Office ergonomics: Your work environment

Working more efficiently will benefit you little if you ruin your health in the process, and the graphic artist's workplace offers a multitude of health hazards, from eyestrain to carpal tunnel syndrome. Setting up your work environment properly will allow you to function more effectively, and to enjoy your work more.

Seating

The right posture is important; your furniture should foster it. A straight back, feet firmly on the floor for support, and elbows bent without strain are what you want. Invest in a decent chair, one that suits your physique. If you choose a stock "office" or "task" chair, it should be fully adjustable in height, seat tilt, and back rest, giving full lumbar support. Some people find that the backless, "kneeling" seating suits them better. There are also "bike seat" chairs that encourage good posture and flexibility. Test before you buy, if possible.

Work station or table

The work surface should be stable and drop low enough for comfortable viewing, keyboarding, and mousing. The height will vary (27 inches is average), so have a friend check your measurements while you are seated in your ergonomic chair: elbows to floor, floor to tops of thighs. Allow plenty of room for legs, thighs, and free movement. Consider such items as articulated keyboard shelves, monitor risers, and adjustable table tops. Armed with your measurements, space requirements, and list of features, shop the computer catalogs, magazines, and retail stores.

Listen to your body and be prepared to change your setup if you notice continuing discomfort; that's a warning sign.

Input devices

Although the keyboard and mouse are ubiquitous, the input device used is a matter of personal preference and work style.

The type of mouse pad you use influences the mouse's tracking ability, as well as your own comfort. It should not be thick enough to force your wrist into an awkward angle. Fabric pads tend to offer more traction, but are harder to clean and can leave solid deposits in the trackball, requiring eventual mouse-cleaning. Hard-surface pads are easier to keep clean, but offer slightly less traction than fabric.

Wrist rests can help to stave off carpal tunnel syndrome. They come in a variety of thicknesses and sizes, from full keyboard to mouse pad. A rolled-up towel works fine, too!

If space is at a premium, a trackball device can be a good option, but it makes a poor drawing tool. So does the mouse; a digitizing tablet may be a better choice for art-related work. Tablets are extremely versatile and have a more natural feel than a mouse. The smaller (up  to 6 x 9 inches), less expensive sizes are adequate for most purposes. For work involving hand-sketching and simu-lated natural media, such options as vinyl tracing overlays and a larger surface may justify the higher price. Pressure sensitivity and erasure are desirable for such applications as retouching and calligraphic work.

Posture

Back: Angled slightly backward to widen angle between torso and thighs, increase blood flow, deepen breathing, and ease compression on spine.

Arms: Relaxed and loose at sides. Forearms and hands parallel to floor.

Thighs: Angled slightly down from torso, transferring some of torso's weight to legs and feet.

Knees: At right angle to thighs.

Chair

Back rest: Supports lower back, matching curve.

Seat: Incline forward slightly to transfer some weight pressure from back to legs and feet.

Cushion: Curves down at front to reduce pressure on thighs.

Arms: Out of elbows' way, allowing full movement of arms. Should be adjustable and removable.

Controls: Should adjust height and tilt angle of back rest and seat, allowing both flexible and locked positions.

Base and feet: Should offer plenty of stability (5-spoke base is best), swivel, and rolling casters. A chair mat allows free movement of the chair.

Eyes

Find a comfortable viewing distance (generally 18 to 28 inches). If you wear bifocals, consider a pair of computer glasses with limited focal range and anti-glare coating.

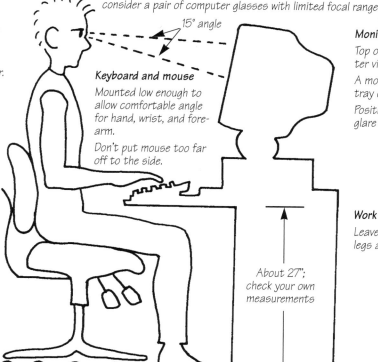

15° angle

Keyboard and mouse

Mounted low enough to allow comfortable angle for hand, wrist, and forearm.

Don't put mouse too far off to the side.

Monitor

Top of screen at eye level, center viewed at about 15° angle.

A monitor stand with keyboard tray can be useful here.

Position monitor to minimize glare from lights and windows.

Work surface

Leave plenty of clearance for legs and feet

About 27"; check your own measurements

Feet

Flat on floor, partially supporting the body's weight.

Hands

Position mouse area so that hand can be held like this...

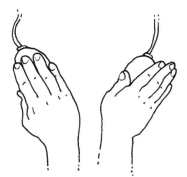

...not like this.

Mouse surface height should be at a comfortable level...

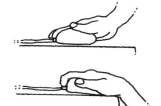

...so wrists are not forced to bend.

Keyboard should allow typing with level wrists...

...rather than bent wrists.

Healthy work habits

Having the right furniture is only part of the solution to work-related health problems. Equally important is the development of healthy practices. And they're free.

Take hourly breaks. Get up, move around, stretch. Go outside and get some sun in your eyes.

When you take a break, do some shoulder and head rolls to loosen up frozen muscles. Try unfocusing and refocusing your eyes several times and roll them around to ease eyestrain and muscle fatigue.

Do a few waist rolls and flex your back. With your feet set shoulder-width apart, slowly slump forward, then roll downward until your torso and arms are hanging limply; then slowly roll back up. This will help to prevent stress buildup in your lower back.

If you notice symptoms that could be repetitive-stress related (sore wrists, swelling, numbness, etc,), don't delay getting treatment. Repetitive stress injuries are easiest to treat when caught early.

Other health aids

For sore wrists, a musician's glove, such as the type sold by Handeeze, can offer support, promote healing, and help to prevent further injury.

Coordinating keyboard and input device for faster input

You can use CE Software's QuicKeys utility to redefine any key on the keyboard for use with your favorite software. For example, set up a numeric keypad to control commonly used commands in your drawing program. You can then work a mouse or tablet with your drawing hand, and issue commands with the other, avoiding menus and two-handed commands and allowing uninterrupted drawing.

Exercises to limber up hands, wrists, and fingers

Massage both sides of hand with thumb and fingers.

Grasp fingers and gently pull back, stretching wrist. Hold for 5 seconds.

Slowly pull thumb down and back until you feel the stretch. Hold for 5 seconds.

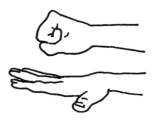

Clench fist, hold a few seconds, and release, fanning fingers out. Repeat 5 times.

Recycling for economy and ecology

The computer industry is a major offender when it comes to toxic waste, wasteful packaging, and general environmental mayhem. Electronic publishing, far from heralding the paperless society, generates mountains of paper printouts. In addition to the potential impact on our ecosystem, the cost of all those sheets of laser paper adds up quickly.

Instead of sending all that paper to some landfill, recycle it. Place two boxes by your printer; label one REUSE and the other RECYCLE. When your printer spits out a blank or mostly blank sheet, drop it into the Reuse box. When the box fills up, reuse the blank sheets in your printer or copier. When you print out a page you don't need to keep but can't reuse, put it into the Recycle box, along with other office papers, junk mail, etc. You'll be amazed at how quickly those boxes fill up.

Try using recycled laser paper, made by a number of paper mills, including Simpson, Hopper, and Weyerhaeuser. Recycled copier paper may work, too. Experiment by getting a few sample sheets from your paper supplier and printing out test pages.

To save additional paper, you can program your printer not to print out test sheets each time it is turned on. You can often adjust the amount of toner it uses, too.

Consider recycling your printer's toner cartridges; savings can be significant. Check the backs of computer magazines for mail-order toner cartridge remanufacturers.

Outdated samples from paper mills make great mountings for portfolio samples. Spray-mount or rubber-cement the art to the paper and slip it into a sleeve, or laminate it in plastic for protection. Smaller outdated swatch books make great message pads.

How to save printer toner and improve print quality

On a laser printer equipped with a toner density control dial, try turning to the lightest setting. You will use less toner and get a crisper, cleaner printout.

Saving money on print or film output

It usually costs less for one 11 x 17-inch page of paper, film, or color proof output than for two 8 1/2 x 11-inch pages. With page layouts that fit the size format, you can ask your service bureau to output your two-page file on one tabloid-size page. This will also allow you to produce bleeds that extend across a spread.

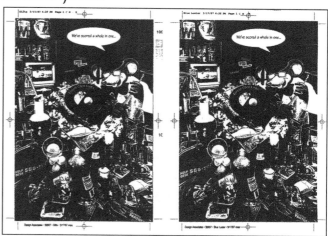

Color in Electronic Publishing
Ensuring accurate color

The accurate specification and production of color for printing from the desktop is challenging; some potential problems are inherent in the process.

The first is screen representation of colors. You are trying to get from RGB "additive" colors (the red, green, and blue produced by your monitor) to the "subtractive" colors of printers' inks. Even when you begin with a CMYK image (such as a photo to retouch), your software translates that image to RGB for screen representation (see page 86, fig. 4). It is usually an imperfect translation, even on a "calibrated" system. Therefore, appraising and matching colors on screen is subject to error.

Compensating for screen representation inaccuracies

If you want your end product to be ink on paper (reflective color), it is best to refer to a reflective model rather than the projected color of the monitor.

If you are working with spot colors (such as Pantone inks), refer to an appropriate spot color swatch book to get a more accurate look at how your color will print on a given paper stock.

If you are working with CMYK colors, keep a CMYK color chart handy (printed on the type of stock—coated or uncoated—that you plan to use) and refer to it when specifying process formulas. When working with a scanned image, you will get a slightly more accurate view of how the image will print if you convert it from RGB to CMYK in your image-editing program, saving the file as a CMYK TIFF. You will, however, also wind up with a much larger file. It is best to make all color adjustments in this program, rather than using the color capabilities of a page layout program; less will be lost in the translation, and the corrections will stay with the original.

For greatest accuracy in color matching and correction in Photoshop, do not rely on the monitor image. Instead, sample the color you wish to match with the Eyedropper tool, and compare its CMYK formula in the Info palette with the formula you are matching to.

If you need to translate a Pantone color to CMYK, and your software will not do this for you, you can refer to a Pantone formula book, or come close by matching to a CMYK chart or swatch book.

If you are trying to match colors, retouching, or creating color-critical original art, you should let an accurate color proof be your final guide, and then re-adjust your color electronically based on the proof, if necessary. The proof may take the form of an Iris or a Rainbow printout, a Matchprint or Cromalin proof, or another prepress method. If you want accuracy, do not rely on color laser or inkjet output as proof. An accurate proof is worth the cost; it may save you more money and disappointment. A press run of 10,000 people with unintended greenish faces is an expensive way of proofing!

Remember to light your work area and color samples well, with as neutral a light as possible, when working with color.

Color shifts, sometimes dramatic ones, occur when an image is converted to a different color space, such as from RGB to CMYK or Pantone to CMYK. Colors that appear bright on the monitor may turn lackluster when translated to colors reproducible in print. You may need to do some tweaking after the conversion, to compensate (see page 86, fig. 5).

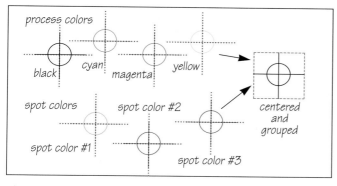

Fig. 1. Making registration marks.

Fig. 2. Different blacks overprinting a 30M 100Y tint.

Fig. 3. Process color blends.

Fig. 4. Overprinting type in black only.

Fig. 5. From top: Type reversed out of solid black, reversed out of black with red (100M 100Y) fill, reversed out of black with 60% yellow fill, reversed out of a process color tint.

Fig. 6. Two quick embossed type effects.

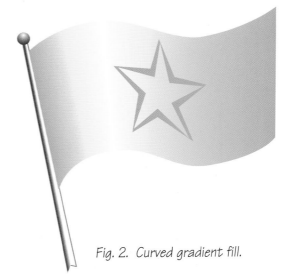

Fig. 2. Curved gradient fill.

Fig. 1. Top: Type mask over photo image.
Bottom: Type filled with photo image.

Fig. 3. Type vignette.

Fig. 4. Hand-drawn lettering, scanned and manipulated in a drawing (left) and painting (right) program.

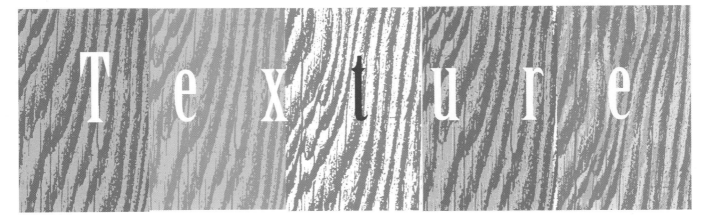

Fig. 5. Bitmapped texture with various shade and background treatments.

Fig. 1. Bitmap TIFF image, showing transparent "white" area.

Fig. 2. Custom screen effects: TIFF halftones, superimposed (left); EPS with clipping path, placed over a TIFF (right).

Fig. 3. Screen effect used as a channel mask in a bitmap image file.

Fig. 4. Vector-drawn text wrapping a bitmapped image.

Fig. 5. Duotone of black and cyan.

Fig. 6. Duotone of black and magenta.

Fig. 1. Line art, colorized and refined.

Shadow

Shadow

Fig. 2. Color-image-to-line-art conversion.

Fig. 3. Drop shadow effects.

Fig. 1. Glow effect.

Fig. 2. Photo vignette.

Fig. 3. Three photo framing devices.

Fig. 4. Ghosted images with text overprinted.

Fig. 1. Selective colorization.

Fig. 2. Embossed effect.

Fig. 3. Isolating an area of a photo.

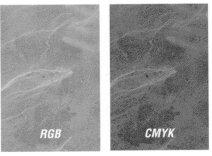

RGB   CMYK

Fig. 4. RGB and CMYK colors compared.

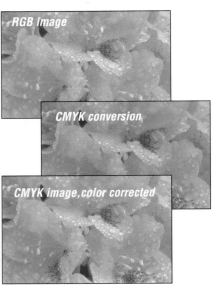

RGB image

CMYK conversion

CMYK image, color corrected

Fig. 5. Conversion from RGB to CMYK.

Cyan 105°
Yellow 90°
Magenta 75°
Black 45°

CMYK screen angles

Moiré, enlarged

Two-color tint enlarged (left) and actual size (right)

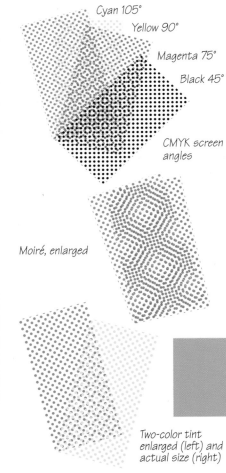

Fig. 6. Screen angles and moiré patterns.

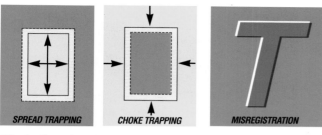

Fig. 1. Trapping versus misregistration on press.

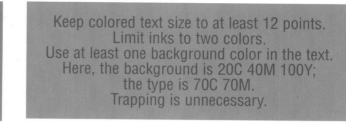

Fig. 2. CMYK type overprinting.

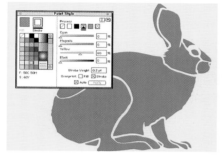

Fig. 3. Trapping line art in a draw program.

Fig. 4. Color correction: adjusting the photo's levels.

Fig. 5. Enhancing detail with unsharp masking.

Fig. 7. Photo retouched with Burn and Dodge tools.

Fig. 6. Color-to-black-and-white conversion.

Fig. 1. Three duotone settings.

Fig. 2. Original grayscale image.

Fig. 3. Duotone EPS layered on grayscale TIFF.

Fig. 4. Image with clipping path imported to a tint background.

Fig. 5. Selectively applied filter.

How to make a viewer for color work

As with any form of color work on the desktop, you need to have a source outside your monitor to reference for accurate color in transparencies. To make a handy transparency viewer, wrap a 2-inch-wide strip of Velcro around a corner of your monitor. Attach another strip to a small portable light box from a camera supply store, and mount it on the monitor. You will have a convenient and accurate way to compare colors.

As an aid for color matching, hang a process color chart in your work area, lit with a full-spectrum light. These charts are often available from printers who do four-color work.

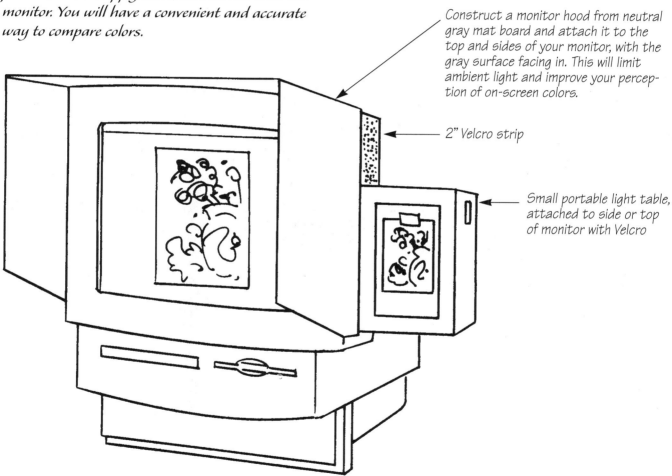

Construct a monitor hood from neutral gray mat board and attach it to the top and sides of your monitor, with the gray surface facing in. This will limit ambient light and improve your perception of on-screen colors.

2" Velcro strip

Small portable light table, attached to side or top of monitor with Velcro

Calibrating your monitor with Photoshop

Any attempt to calibrate a monitor should begin with following the instructions in the Photoshop manual. Once this process is completed, some further fine-tuning is possible.

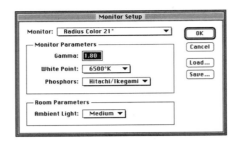 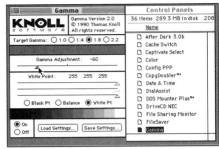

Begin by making sure your monitor's specifications are selected in Photoshop's Monitor Setup box under the Preferences menu. Adjust the gamma using the gamma control panel.

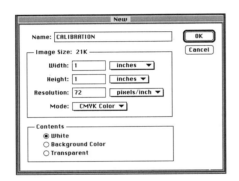 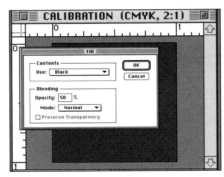 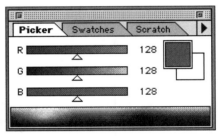

To tweak the monitor setup, create a small CMYK file and fill it with 50% black. Using the Eyedropper tool, sample the gray fill.

Show the Color Picker palette and set it to display RGB values. These should all show values of 128. If they are not, go to File/Preferences/Monitor Setup and adjust the gamma setting. Go back to your CMYK document and check the RGB values again. Repeat these steps until you read 128 for R, G, and B.

PostScript and color output: Avoiding moiré patterns

PostScript has some limitations when reproducing color halftones. Imagesetters output film set at specific screen angles for producing halftones composed of two or more colors. The customary angles are: cyan 90, magenta 75, yellow 90, and black 45 degrees. When combined, the dot patterns of all four inks form the familiar and desirable rosette, which the eye tends to read as a continuous tone. When any of the angles are even slightly off, moiré patterns can form (see page 86, fig. 6). The eye picks these up as obtrusive dot patterns in the printed image. Usually, the black plate is the cause.

A few simple techniques decrease the likelihood of moirés and other registration problems:

Process colors composed of three or more inks stand a greater chance of causing moirés; specify only two inks if possible.

Use a single, solid color to print small text (under 10 point) and rules less than .5 point in thickness; set these elements to overprint background colors.

Halftone dot patterns sometimes conflict with patterns in the image itself, such as fine checks or plaids in fabric. Here it may help to do some color correction, reducing the amount of black in the pattern area and adjusting the other inks to compensate.

Avoid overriding the screen rulings and angles specified by the application's PPD files; they are calculated to minimize moiré patterns.

The way to check for unwanted dot patterns is to order a prepress proof produced from the final film, such as a Matchprint, which shows the actual dot patterns together. If you have only a few images that might cause trouble, you can economize by having these images output as a random proof on one page.

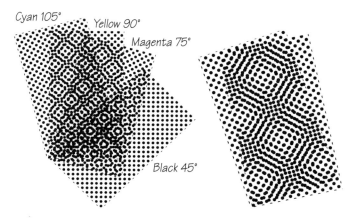

Cyan 105° Yellow 90° Magenta 75° Black 45°

Correct screen angles applied to ink colors result in an unobstusive rosette pattern.

When screen angles are even slightly off, a moiré pattern is produced.

Moirés are much easier to control in tints composed of only two ink colors.

.5 point rule

In general, .5 point rules or smaller, and 10 point type or smaller should be specified as a single solid color and set to overprint.

Troubleshooting
Memory error messages

If you are trying to perform a task in a Mac application and you get an "almost out of memory" message, it could be caused by a large item recently copied to the clipboard, hogging memory. Try selecting a single character (in a word processing or page layout program) or a very small part of an image (in a draw or image-editing program) and copy it to the clipboard. Now repeat this step. The first step replaces the larger item in the clipboard; the second removes it from a temporary buffer, making a much smaller clipboard and freeing up more memory. Now try to perform the task again.

If you still get a memory problem message, save the file and quit the application, as well as any others that may be running. Select the application's icon, choose Get Info from the File menu, and see mow much memory has been allotted for the application. Try increasing the minimum and preferred amounts, reopening the application and file you were working on, and performing the operation again.

Another possibility: if you have over 8 megabytes of RAM installed, check the memory control panel under the Apple menu to make sure that 32-bit addressing is on; if not, turn it on and restart. With 32-bit addressing, you can install and access much more RAM, too.

You can also activate virtual memory in the memory control panel, borrowing some hard disk space to augment available RAM, but this may slow your application considerably. However, with 128 megabytes of RAM installed, you can access up to a gigabyte of virtual memory, plenty to handle large color files. With most Mac models, 32-bit addressing must be on.

If you consistently get "out of memory" messages, it may be time to add some RAM.

Maximizing disk storage space

A PC/Windows system needs disk space for a permanent swap file of at least 12 megabytes for graphics-intensive programs.

Defragmenting your hard drive periodically can help your system to make maximum use of available memory. You can use a disk optimization utility like Norton Utilities to do this while you're having lunch.

Keep 5 to 10% of your hard drive free for temporary files created by applications; then check for redundant temporary files, which can eat up usable space.

You can maximize your available disk space simply by being judicious in the way you save files.

For instance, the Indexed Color option in Photoshop creates far smaller files than the RGB or CMYK formats. You can do your editing work in an original CMYK file, save it, then resave it as an Indexed Color image, setting the palette to Adaptive and resolution to 256 colors. This file can be used as an FPO or to print a comp, and will take up much less room and printing time than the original. To make it even smaller, reduce the image resolution (say, from 300 ppi to 72 ppi—fine for on-screen use).

A draw program file saved in its native format rather than as an EPS will be considerably smaller.

You can control the size of PostScript files in Windows applications by specifying the printer driver used to create the file. A file created for a laser printer will be much more compact than one intended for an imagesetter. The driver called PostScript Printer on File offers the most options.

Recovering from a crash

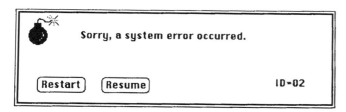

Sorry, a system error occurred.

[Restart] [Resume] ID=02

The Mac's crash error messages are not of much use unless you are a technician, and can simply serve to irritate you by telling you what you already know.

If you suspect that extension conflicts may have caused the crash, turn them off upon restart by holding down the Shift key. You will need to restart again to turn them back on. An extension control utility like Extensions Manager or Conflict Catcher can help you to isolate problem extensions by turning off extensions selectively.

If an application hangs on your Mac and causes it to freeze, try typing Command/Option/Escape. You lose any unsaved work in the document you were working on, but can at least return to the desktop and save any other open files. After a forced quit, it is a good idea to restart before continuing.

If this trick does not work, the next technique is to press the reset switch on the Mac's case, which will force the Mac to restart. Consult the manual for the location of this switch on the model you use. The last, and least desirable, move is to turn the Mac off and then back on again with the power switch, which causes the hard drive to reboot. Since crashes happen without warning, use the Save command frequently.

The PC version of crash recovery is the "three-finger salute": press Control/Alt/Delete. This may return you to your program and allow you to continue working.

Electronic Prepress
Working with a service bureau, prepress shop, or printer

Finding a supplier

Interview prospective suppliers using these criteria, in this order: skill, experience, craftsmanship, price, technology. Lowest price and slickest equipment don't always produce best value.

Tour the shop; is it clean, well organized? Ask for a list of services and equipment. Capabilities, output resolutions? Does the shop offer color proofs? What kind? What is the pricing structure? What is normal turnaround time? Can it take files by modem and assist in that process? Assist in troubleshooting? Will it stand behind its work or pass the problems back to you? Are pickup and delivery offered? Is training provided? Does the staff appear skilled and tasteful (look at work samples)? Are they willing to share information? Will you be assigned your own service rep? What file formats, software, and media can they work with? Ask for references and check them.

Working together

You may think your suppliers work for you, but in fact they work with you. You want them on your side, so establish a personal relationship from the start. It will open the lines of communication and help to smooth the rough spots. Eventually, you will develop a feel for working together and the more routine jobs may need little preliminary discussion.

For a first project or any job of any size or complexity, hold a preflight planning session before you start production. Give as many details about the job as you can. Establish the roles everyone is to play, including the extent of your involvement. Ask for advice on file construction. Discuss incidentals like shipping costs and last-minute changes.

Send representative test files to check for potential output problems. Include any recurring graphics, or those that signal possible trouble (such as blends), on a page with selected text in the fonts to be used. Have the page output as a prepress proof and check it for trouble areas. Often this is done as part of the service package.

Allow extra time for wrenches in the works. Even though a file prints out flawlessly on your laser printer, it can still give trouble to the imagesetter. If you have trouble printing it, your supplier probably will, too!

Work digitally, communicate traditionally with printers. Many of the effects generated on the desktop were recently done in a traditional darkroom or stripping department; some will still be worked on in these settings. Printing is still largely an analog medium.

Supplying your own film

The best advice for supplying film to the printer is _don't_. Usually, the more quality-control elements under one roof, the better; for consistency and accountability and, often, for best price. If you must supply film, know the printer's requirements (ask for a specification sheet if possible). Better, have the supplier communicate directly with the film source.

Some film specs you will need:

❖ Emulsion direction; in the United States, final film negatives are usually right reading, emulsion down (RRED).

❖ Line screen resolution; depends on press and paper; usually ranges from 40 lpi (for silk screen printing) to 200 lpi and up (for sheet-fed offset).

❖ Imagesetter resolution; depends on the equipment's capabilities; usually from 1,200 to 3,386 dpi.

Other elements you may need to consider:

❖ Dot gain; dependent on press and paper. Halftone dots tend to expand when laid down on paper, and compensation must be made in the film.

❖ Dot shape: round, square, elliptical.

Preparing files for processing by a service bureau or printer

The number-one recurrent problem for service bureaus is the discovery that fonts and images are missing from files destined for output. Double-check your files before you send them. To help with this, use software aids like Quark's Collect for Output feature under the File menu. This command creates a report that lists all fonts and graphic files used in a document. You can customize the format of these reports and print them out to send along with your files as a guide to the printer.

Routinely check your documents before they go out

❖ Check the page layout document to make sure all imported graphics are in place and updated.

❖ Check the color palette in your page layout document to make sure that all colors used in imported graphics are in the list, correctly named. Delete all unnecessary colors, including Red, Green, and Blue.

❖ Check EPS and TIFF files; make sure that all necessary clipping paths are included, that all resolutions are correct. Don't rename a graphic file once it has been placed in another file; if you do, be sure to update the file where it was placed.

Quark's Collect for Output feature generates a document report, listing fonts, graphics, and colors used in the file, to print out for reference. It also copies all graphic files linked to the document and saves them to the file transport disk.

Keep your files as clean and small as possible

❖ Eliminate unnecessary control points in vector paths; too many of these cause limitcheck (memory) errors on RIP devices. A common villain here is Photoshop's Make Path command. When used with a Magic Wand tool selection, this command can generate far too many control points. Use the Path Pen tool instead. To clean up a path in Illustrator, use the Pathfinder/Unite filter on the selected path.

❖ Delete unnecessary items rather than covering them up with white rectangles.

❖ Keep processing time down by avoiding many complex blends, limiting them to a few simple shapes.

❖ Scale and rotate scanned or bitmapped images in their software of origin, saving them to repro size, rather than scaling or rotating them in a page layout program. This cuts down on file size and processing time and ensures correct resolution. An easy approach: scale and rotate your image in a page layout application, jot down the angle and percentages, and apply these to the original images file, then reimport the file.

❖ Vector-based art may be scaled, rotated, and skewed in a page layout with no loss of output quality. Be aware, however, that stroke widths will be altered by scaling.

❖ Use EPS and TIFF formats for graphic images imported as live art (intended for output "as-is"); PICT format is not recommended.

❖ Do not save Photoshop EPS files containing halftone screens with transfer function activated; the image-setter will determine these settings.

❖ JPEG, LZW, and other image file compression formats may not be supported by the output system; check before using them.

Troubleshoot in advance

Whenever possible, do some preflight troubleshooting with the prepress department.

Describe the job, the graphics it will contain, the software you plan to use. Ask if any of the software or file type could pose some problems, and how to avoid them.

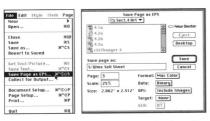 A Quark document page can be saved as an EPS for output or for import to another application. Just be sure to include all embedded fonts or images when sending the file. This is an effective way to keep the page intact, since it cannot be changed or edited. However, this can also create problems; check with your supplier first.

Embedded files

Embedding files and fonts into one another is also called "nesting." Be careful how many embedded files you nest; nesting more than two levels deep can cause output problems. Rather than embedding fonts in an EPS imported into a page layout, create the type in the page layout. Or convert the type to outlines before exporting.

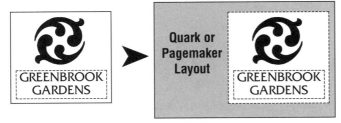

Type "nested" in an EPS file should be converted to outlines before import to a page layout. Alternatively, create all type in the page layout.

DCS files

DCS (Desktop Color Separation) files are the form electronic publishing documents (such as CMYK TIFF files) convert to before they are processed in an imagesetter. Since DCS files can take up more than five times the disk space of the original files, it is best to let the printer or service bureau do the conversion after the files are transported; this will also allow any other necessary file manipulation to be done by the supplier.

CMYK TIFF files need to be converted to DCS format for high-resolution output, but this can increase their size by four to five times. Send the files unconverted, and let the prepress facility do the conversion.

DCS files cannot be sent through a Scitex RIP. If your prepress service uses this equipment, save your files with the DCS option inactive.

DCS image files are not supported by some applications (for example, Quark will accept them; Illustrator will not).

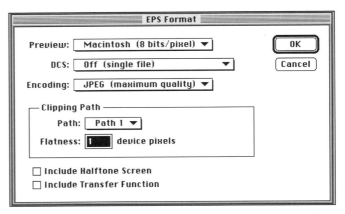

Photoshop's EPS Format Save dialog box; note that DCS file encoding is off.

File preparation tips

Here are some general guidelines to help ensure trouble-free file processing and output by a service bureau or printer.

❖ Include all graphics referenced in the file, including those embedded in other graphic files. Provide a list of graphics and their formats, and the applications/versions used to create them.

❖ Supply or list all fonts (including full name, vendor, and type). Remember those embedded in EPS files (or convert those to outlines).

❖ Send clean files. Delete unused items from pasteboards, unused colors, graphics, and fonts, and save as a final "output" version of the file.

❖ Organize your files on the transfer medium. Create folders on the floppy, SyQuest, or Zip named for their contents, and sort the document files into them: fonts, graphics, document for output. Set them up logically, so anyone can access them easily. Print out two copies of the disk directory; keep one and send the other attached to the disk.

❖ Create a README file to travel with your document, preferably in the page layout program in which the document was composed. Otherwise, use SimpleText or a common word processor. Include any instructions pertinent to the document: fonts and spot colors used, line-screen, resolution, page sizes, etc. List the files to be output (easy way: print out the window of the folder containing the files, or select all and paste into your README document). Detail any additional work needed before output: note whether trapping needs to be done, or if it has been done already. Designate the medium you want output: film, RC paper, Iris proof, etc., and

the manner in which you want the output: positive/negative, direction reading, size %, with or without crops. Specify reader spreads (pages arranged in their numerical order) or printer spreads (arranged in printers' forms or imposition), individual pages, or imposed flats. List the number of plates to be output for color separations. For print jobs, include all specs: paper stocks, inks, bleeds, folds or perfs, and size of press run. Be sure to include your name and phone number in case of questions or problems. Print out two copies: one to send, one to keep.

❖ Supply at least a laser printout of the entire document, at 100% if possible. If you are having separations output, include one composite printout and one set of all color plates. Make hand-written notations on the printout if necessary for clarification; send a copy and keep one.

❖ Double-check everything before it goes out to verify that everything required to output the job is in place.

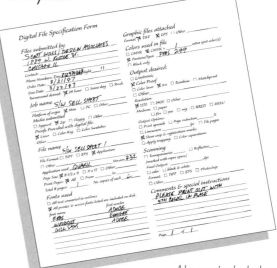

Always include hard-copy documentation with your files.

TrueType icon

Do not use system fonts and TrueType fonts for imagesetter output. To confirm which fonts are TrueType, view them by icon. The "triple A" fonts are TrueType. To make sure they are deactivated, remove them from your system folder. Use only PostScript fonts. Non-PostScript fonts (like Chicago, Geneva, or the other city-name system fonts) will print out as bitmaps.

Always send a complete set of screen and printer fonts for output. Removing fonts from a suitcase will cause type to reflow because of the alteration to the suitcase. The small amount of disk space saved is not worth the potential problem.

Avoid font substitution systems such as Super ATM; they replace actual fonts with artificial ones, without notifying you.

Always apply style attributes such as Bold or Italic by using the actual typeface, rather than by selecting the attributes from a menu. This will ensure correct output.

"Bolding" a bold face is not a good idea, either. Imagesetters will produce inconsistent results. But if the font you are using does not have the weight you want, you can fake it for short text. Here's how:

Create the text in a draw program using the font you want. Once you have it in the configuration you need, convert the text to outlines and group it. If you want it bold, give the text a slight

Mark your instructions on laser proofs in red; use neon highlighters. Make them impossible to miss! You can also tape tissue overlays on to hold your notes.

stroke in whatever color the type is to print. If you want it light, give it a slight white stroke (for a white background). Then manually adjust the letterspacing for the proper look.

Define line weights as .25 point or greater. "Hairline" settings can output differently on different devices, and may be too thin to print. This applies to borders, too.

.25 point line, output at 1270 dpi ————————
Hairline, output at 1270 dpi ————————

Outline text should be created in a postscript draw program. Type in the text and give it the stroke color you want. This allows maximum flexibility and correct output.

When defining CMYK colors, name them as formulas rather than descriptive names: "30 cyan 5 magenta (or 30C 5M)" instead of "logo blue." Stick to 5% increments when defining tints of an ink color.

When defining process colors, make sure the Process Separation feature is active so the color will separate properly. It should be turned off for spot colors unless you want the imagesetter to substitute the process color equivalent.

Never apply a tint to a four-color process color. That is, do not create a pink from 100M 100Y by applying a 50% tint; use a formula of 50M 50Y at 100%.

If you expect the printer to match a color, include a swatch for reference with your instructions.

When marking up photos to be scanned and dropped into a page layout, give each photo a logically sequenced name, corresponding to any images already placed in the file. Example: FPO (For Position Only) photo 1C goes on page 1 along with EPS 1A and TIFF 1B. Mark each photo on the back or transparent sleeve in grease pencil or indelible marker, never ballpoint pen or pencil, to avoid marring the emulsion surface.

Mark all placed artwork or effects (such as blends) to be output directly from your file as LIVE.

Reflective art that is to be scanned must fit on a drum scanner. This means it needs to be a flexible medium (no thicker than 12-point cover stock), probably no larger than 20" x 24" (check with your printer). If your art will not fit, you need to have a photo transparency shot.

When you send revised files for output, be sure to give them names different from the original files. Add a prefix or suffix to the original name, such as "Brochure Rev." or "Brochure R1." Multiple revisions call for sequential name additions: "Rev 1," "Rev 2," and so on. Be sure to accompany revised files with printouts from those files, with clear instructions.

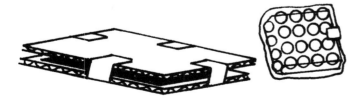

Pack photos and flat art carefully, sandwiched between rigid materials like corrugated board, to protect them from bending, creasing, or shipping damage. Pack disks and cartridges carefully, too, with plenty of padding.

Sending electronic media through the mail is risky. If you must, however, print "Magnetic Media Enclosed" on the package to prevent your files from being damaged or erased by postal machinery.

For consistency and time savings, make up custom labels for your file transport media. Stock label forms are available from office suppliers and printers; you can photocopy or laser-print your own or have them offset-printed. Or use a rubber-stamp.

If you send compressed image files to conserve space, save them as SEA (self-extracting) files. That way, they will open at the other end, even if the decompression software is lacking.

If the document is to print to any or all edges (bleed), you need to include a bleed area on your page layout. Different printers ask for different bleed amounts, anywhere from 1/8" to 3/8". If in doubt, provide a 3/8" bleed.

When preparing DOS/Windows files for PostScript output, select a PostScript printer driver such as Apple Laserwriter or Linotronic before starting the document. If you do this after the document is done, text and graphics may reflow. You could also change the Windows Default Printer to Linotronic or Laserwriter instead of Applications Printer, restart, and apply the Use Windows Printer option. Remember to restore your normal driver when finished.

If the file is made into a PostScript Print-to-File EPS, select Make Separations in the print setup before selecting Print toFile. The correct number of EPS plates will be created. Make sure color is defined as CMYK to produce correct screen angles. Line screen/resolution should also be set up before the file is constructed.

When one vignette file is laid on top of another, you will frequently get an unwanted jagged edge around the topmost one at output. Two solutions: the easiest is to add a keyline around the top vignette in your page layout. It will remove the jaggies, but give you a harder edge. To retain the soft edge, combine the two files in an image-editing program.

Page imposition software used in high-end systems will sometimes renumber pages; check proofs carefully!

If you need to correct one plate in a multicolor job, have a full set of negatives rerun, for all the colors. This will guard against misregister or color shifts caused by subtle differences in film output under different environmental conditions.

When your document is finished, check it to make sure all placed images are current. In Quark, use the Picture Usage menu.

To double-check, open and print the document from the media used to transport the file for output; if there are any missing graphics files, you will be able to tell from on-screen alert messages or incorrectly printed images.

Using APR

APR (Automatic Picture Replacement), also called OPI (Open Press Interface), is a method of swapping high-resolution for low-resolution image files during processing by an imagesetter. Here's how it works.

When you send photos or artwork to be scanned and saved on high-end equipment, low-resolution versions of the high-resolution files are saved and sent to you. You place the low-resolution files in your page layout, send the layout files to the imagesetter, and the high-resolution files (which have the same file names as the low-res ones) are substituted by the output system.

There are several advantages to this procedure. It saves you the time of working with the high-resolution files, and the disk space required to store them. The high-resolution images can be color-corrected, retouched, or otherwise manipulated by experts while you are placing the low-resolution versions in your layout, cropped as desired.

Here are a few caveats. APR requires you to measure and provide accurate proportional and positioning specifications for the scans; you will have no more than 20% leeway in sizing the scanned images in your layout. The closer to actual reproduction size, the better. If you must resize the image more than 120% or less than 80%, have it rescanned. Rotating the scanned image in the layout may cause output problems; have the scanning done at the correct angle of rotation. When you receive the low-resolution files, do not rename them. Changing the names will break the link with the high-resolution files, and no swapping will take place. Likewise, do not resave the low-res image in a different format.

Checklist for prepress-ready electronic files

Make sure your files meet all the following requirements before sending them to your supplier. Indicate this in your transmittal memo. Your printer or service bureau may have its own checklist; if so, use it. If not, here's one you can use as a guide. Copy this list, make up your own to print out with each job, or use the sample transmittal form on the following page.

❖ Platform used (Mac or PC) and all software used to create files, including version numbers, are noted.

❖ All documents for output are included (save a backup copy). If you send multiple jobs, make this clear in your notes or a separate transmittal, with files arranged accordingly.

❖ All fonts are PostScript fonts.

❖ Special text effects are properly applied (outlines, shadows, bold, italic, etc.).

❖ All colors are defined correctly:

Black-and-white continuous tone is grayscale.

RGB colors are defined as spot or CMYK. Avoid using red, green, and blue; you may want to delete these from the file's color menu.

CMYK formulas are defined with Separation active.

Pantone colors are converted and defined as CMYK, unless they are printing as spot colors.

Fifth color is defined as spot color (and Separation is turned off).

❖ Colors have the same names in all files.

❖ All graphics files accompany the document they appear in. It is a good idea to send editable versions of the files; this will save time if last-minute changes are necessary.

❖ All fonts (both screen and printer files) accompany the document they appear in, in a folder labeled "Fonts." State that the fonts are included for one-time output only, to honor your license.

❖ Each image to be scanned is marked with instructions.

❖ Every file has a unique name.

❖ Revised files have new names.

❖ Laser proof of final version of document, including all crop marks, at 100% (tile if necessary) is enclosed with files. If proof is not 100%, note % of actual size. If it is a black-and-white proof, print colors as gray.

❖ All FPO images are labeled on laser proofs. (All other images will be considered live art.)

❖ Printed instructions are on proofs submitted, including color instructions, tints, percentages, scans to drop in and their placement, etc.

❖ A folded dummy is included when folding is required.

❖ Menu or directory printout of all files is attached.

❖ A Collect for Output file and printout or equivalent is included.

❖ Files are accompanied by a completed specification form.

❖ All shipping media (floppy, SyQuest, etc.) are labeled with document name, disk number, date, and place of origin. Disks are locked to prevent inadvertent changes or erasure.

Digital file specification form

Files submitted by

_____
_____
_____
Contact: _____
Phone Numbers: Day_____Night_____
Order Date: _____
Due Date: _____
Turnaround desired: ☐ 24 hour ☐ Same day ☐ Rush

Job name

_____
Platform: ☐ Mac ☐ PC ☐ Other_____
Media submitted:
☐ SyQuest ☐ Zip ☐ Floppy ☐ Other_____
Proofs provided with digital file:
☐ Laser ☐ Color Key ☐ Color Swatches
Other _____

File name

_____
File Format: ☐ TIFF ☐ EPS ☐ Application
☐ Other _____
Application used:_____ Version_____
Page Size: ☐ 8 ½ x 11 ☐ 11 x 17 ☐ Other_____
Print Pages: ☐ All ☐ From _____ to _____
Total # pages: _____ No. copies of each_____

Fonts used

☐ All text converted to outlines
☐ All printer & screen fonts listed are included on disk:
font name   font vendor

_____
_____
_____
_____
_____
_____
_____

Graphics files attached

Format: ☐ TIFF ☐ EPS ☐ Other_____

Colors used in file

☐ CMYK ☐ CMYK + _____extra spot color(s)
☐ Pantone/Spot _____
☐ Black only

Output desired

☐ Linotronic
☐ Color Proof
☐ Color laser ☐ Iris ☐ Rainbow ☐ Matchprint ☐ Cromalin
☐ Other_____
Resolution:
☐ 1,270 ☐ 2,400 ☐ Other _____
Medium: ☐ paper ☐ film
☐ pos ☐ neg: ☐ RRED ☐ RREU ☐ other_____
Output Options:
☐ Print spreads ☐ Page reduction_____%
☐ Linescreen _____lpi ☐ Tile pages
☐ Show crop & registration marks
☐ Apply trapping ☐ Color separations

Scanning

☐ Transparencies _____ ☐ Reflective_____
(marked with repro specs)
Final Output: _____dpi
☐ color ☐ black & white
Format: ☐ TIFF ☐ EPS ☐ Photoshop
☐ Other_____

Comments & special instructions

_____
_____
_____
_____
_____
_____
_____

Page_____ of_____

Photoshop settings

Check before adjusting any Photoshop default Preference settings for image files; the printer or publisher may prefer to do all file adjustments. Here are some setting changes to consider. If you are manipulating the image in CMYK mode, new settings will affect only the monitor display. If you are converting to CMYK from RGB or LAB, the image's separation setup will be affected as well.

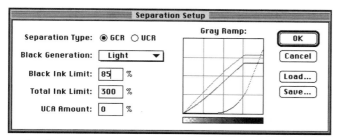

Black Limit

Black Limit (BL) settings determine the amount of black ink that will print in the darkest color. Set it at 75-85%, a good range for a variety of presses.

Total Ink Limit

"Gas-ghosting" occurs when the percentage of combined ink colors from photo image files produces too much coverage on a sheet. When the sheets are stacked, the ink gases are trapped, causing a ghost image to form on the sheets above and below. To avoid this problem, select Separation under Preferences and enter 300 into Total Ink Limit for sheet-fed offset, or 280 for web offset. This will limit the CMYK values in the dark color areas, and minimize the problem. Some publications have strict guidelines for this setting.

Total Ink Coverage (TIC)

Also referred to as maximum density (DMax), TIC should be set between 280 and 320%. This defines the CMYK values allowed for the darkest color. For sheet-

fed offset printing, the TIC should be less than 300%; for web offset, less than 280%. Colors whose components total more than these values may exceed the press's capabilities, producing too-heavy ink coverage.

GCR

Gray Color Replacement substitutes black ink for CMY inks in neutral tones. Use GCR judiciously (Light setting) to retain detail in heavy shadow areas of an otherwise high-toned image.

UCR

Using UCR (or No GCR) concentrates black ink in shadow areas and leaves a lighter black coverage in the details of non-shadow areas. Generally, the setting should be 0 when converting from RGB to CMYK.

Dot Gain

Dot gain occurs on press when the ink in each halftone dot spreads slightly into the surrounding paper. Actually, each dot gains 1-2% in each production stage:

film, plate, press, paper. This means that a 20% tint in your document may print as a 24% tint on coated paper, a 28% tint on uncoated. To compensate, settings entered in software can control dot size in film output to adjust for paper and press conditions. Generally, set the gain at 25% for midquality presswork, such as magazine printing. Adjust lower for high-quality press and paper, higher for newsprint.

Transfer Function

When you save an image file, bypass the Transfer Function; it can throw the imagesetter off, or may simply be preempted by the output system.

Quick fixes

Use conventional paste-up methods to paste a sharp laser printout over a jagged imagesetter output.

An emergency type fix: laser-print the text at 200% and have it reduced to film at 50% and stripped into your lay-out.

Electronic "post-its" make your instructions clear where they might otherwise be missed. You can also leave these notes outside the trim area, but be sure that the note text box overlaps the trim line so it will print out on your laser proofs.

Quick fixes for paper output:

Imagesetters can't smooth out bitmapped images the way laser printers can. If one of your images comes back with the jaggies, you can paste a smoother laser-printed image over it.

If you need to replace a block of type on an RC paper or film printout in a hurry, try printing the type out on your laser printer at 200% size; then have the printer reduce it on film and strip it in. The reduction will help to compensate for different output resolutions.

Place electronic "post-it" notes to call attention to instructions on your page layout or art file. Make a text box, color it solid yellow, and type a message into it, then place it over the art. Instruct the operator to remove it once it has been read! You can also use this technique to label FPO art.

To fix a corrupted Quark file, switch to Thumbnail view and copy all pages in the document to a new file. This also eliminates unused colors, style sheets, and master pages.

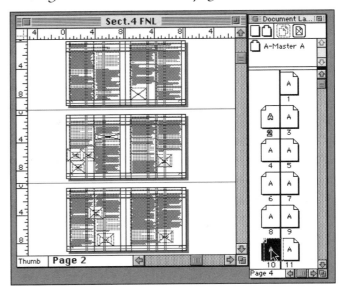

Trapping

When your multicolor job is on press, areas of color that border each other may separate slightly due to press misalignment, paper condition, or any number of reasons. When this happens, slivers of white appear in the gaps between the ink. One way to deal with this potential problem is trapping. When a trap is created in printing film by traditional methods, a color bordering another is made to overlap slightly by increasing its area (spread) or by increasing that of its neighbor (choke or shrink). Sometimes a combination of these is used on the same page (see page 87, fig. 1).

Essentially, trapping is the substitution of one planned defect (the trap) for another potential defect (misregistration). The easiest and most elegant solution is to plan your artwork in such a way as to render trapping unnecessary. Discuss the issue with your printer. If the juxtaposition of colors warrants trapping, more decisions will be required to prevent the cure from being more obtrusive than the problem.

To determine the type and amount of trap needed, you must factor in the page layout, the tolerances of the press to be used, the type of paper stock, inks, and other specifications. The printer is final judge of trapping values, which are a technical as well as an aesthetic consideration. Excessive traps can produce unwanted dark borders around objects. Inadequate traps allow paper show-through.

As a rule of thumb, a trap value of .2 point is needed between two light colors. A larger trap can be tolerated between dark colors, from .25 to .3 points per

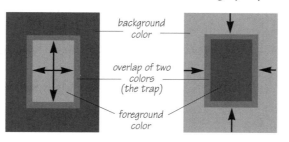

Spread trapping   Choke trapping

color. When black overprints on any of the colors, the trap can be still larger: from .25 to .6 points. Darker colors generally trap to lighter ones; text usually traps to the background.

Screen representation has limitations: potential trapping problem areas are not always readily visible on a monitor. For example, many "trapping" problems are actually "fit" problems, as with images in picture boxes on a page layout. Always leave a bit of extra image behind a box or frame. This avoids the gaps that you cannot see on screen but that show up on press. Also, use grids, guides, and measurements to line up elements on the page, rather than just eyeballing; the screen can lie just enough to throw you off.

A simple way to trap a CMYK document is to use a common process color "bridge" in each neighboring color area. When touching colors have 10% or more or cyan, magenta, yellow, or black in common, a misregistration will be covered by the bridge, preventing any white show-through. This does away with the need to apply spread or choke traps.

Improperly trapped files (or files that are not trapped at all) account for a large percentage of pre-press problems. When they are not caught and corrected, they can ruin a printed piece's appearance.

Here are four options available to address trapping problems: conventional, desktop, high-end, and combination trapping methods. Consider each before deciding on a course of action. As with all prepress issues, discuss options with your printer or prepress person before beginning production.

Conventional trapping is the traditional darkroom stripping method of creating a trap by sandwiching a clear "spacer" between a film negative and unexposed final film. It is straightforward, fast, economical, and versatile. To use this method, it is generally best to provide the printer with paper output, which will be treated like a conventional artboard. This method works best with simple two- and three-color jobs. As with any multicolor job, a color proof or sketch should accompany the artwork, to serve as a guide to pre-press.

Desktop trapping may be manual, automatic, or a combination of both. With desktop trapping, you have more control, but also more responsibility. Desktop methods often require trapping each element of a lay-out in the program used to create it; for example, page layout programs cannot trap EPS files.

Draw programs are most commonly used for manual trapping. To create spread traps, slightly wider stroke values are applied to certain lines and edges, and these are given an Overprint attribute. A choke trap is more complicated. A copy of the fore-ground object is made, pasted between the back-ground and foreground, and stroked with the back-ground color set to Overprint. For objects that are partly overlapping another color and a white area, creating traps is yet more involved. The affected paths need to be cut, and overprinting strokes assigned only to the portions touching the background color. This can be a tedious process with a complex illustration.

Automatic trapping can be done in page layout programs or dedicated programs like Trapwise, using either defaults or customized settings. Caution: Default trap values will not always give the correct trap. Even when a placed EPS is properly trapped, it will need to be redone if the image is resized in a page layout program, because the stroke widths will change. Open the EPS file and resize the image, while activating Keep Stroke Values. Then update the page layout file. Desktop trapping should not be done by the inexperienced, or under a tight deadline with no allowance for errors. Improperly trapped files can usu-ally be corrected by conventional or high-end methods, but will require more time to do so.

High-end trapping is, on first glance, the most costly option. It offers the most sophisticated controls, combining specialized software and hardware with the expertise of prepress CEP specialists. Some shops have hybrid systems, where desktop equipment interfaces with high-end RIPs. Desktop files are converted to bitmapped images by a RIP, so that editing and trap-ping can be done on a pixel-by-pixel level. High-end work is particularly well suited to complex color work and packaging projects. When this method is chosen, provide untrapped desktop files. Shop around among trade shops and service bureaus to find a shop that does high-end system work at desktop prices.

Desktop traps can be checked by printing separa-tions in enlarged size on a laser printer, with registra-tion marks, then using a small light table to view the separations placed on top of each other. To make sure the traps are where they should be, set the trapping amount to a large value (like 20 points) for the proof.

Combination trapping incorporates two or more of the three types. This option is often exercised by print-ers, to utilize the most effective means at their disposal.

Who should do the trapping?

Once you understand trapping and have the software to do it, you are faced with a choice: should you attempt to trap a job yourself, or ask your supplier to do it?

If you decide to do trapping yourself, consult with your printer first. Find out the tolerances of the press, and ask for a recommendation as to how much trap to apply, and which colors should overprint. Start with a simple two-color job before attempting more complex trapping.

There are several advantages in having your printer trap. Most printers and service bureaus have specialized software running on high-end systems for trapping electronic files. Specialized programs such as Trapwise, Full AutoFrame, and Trapper can do trapping much more effectively than most lower-end programs, and offer options unavailable with traditional methods. They have the benefit of highly skilled staff who trap colors all day long, and who can also revert to conventional darkroom work for trapping, if necessary. There will probably be little, if any, additional cost for this, and it places the responsibility on experts. Be sure it is clear who is doing the trapping. If it is the printer, be aware that an EPS file embedded in a page layout file cannot be trapped. The EPS must be opened and trapped independently, so be sure to include that file when sending materials for output.

If you do the trapping...
Here are a few basic guidelines.

There are alternatives to trapping. In process work, you can use bridge colors. You can apply no trap at all, and simply apply a knockout (one color reverses out of another with no overlap imposed), trusting that press misregistration will be minimal.

You can overprint the (darker) foreground color on the (lighter) background color, as is customary with black type.

When applying a trap, remember that the trap should be hidden in the darker color. For example, if you have a deep purple object against a light yellow background (or vice versa), the trap should spread into the purple, making it less visible. In the case of two colors with similar values, the trap may be divided between them, minimizing the trap's overlap line.

If only a few page elements need trapping, such as headlines, create these in a draw program and assign overprinting strokes to the objects or type, then import them into the page layout program. Be sure to double an overprinting stroke width; strokes generated in vector-based programs are centered on an object's outside border. Only half of the stroke width will overlap the adjacent color area.

For simple jobs, turn off the page layout's default trapping feature in Preferences. Then trap only those page elements that need it, individually, through the trapping dialog box. For more complex jobs, apply general trapping and fix individual problems.

Suggested Trapping Amounts	
1-color press (local quick-print shop), offset paper	0.4 point
2-color press	0.23 point
High-quality press, coated stock	0.15 point
Silk screen or Flexographic press	1.0 point

How to create a trap for line art in a draw program

To produce proper trapping on a line-art image placed into a tint on a page layout, follow these steps. Illustrator was used in this example.

1. Consider your color choices and decide which color will trap to which. In this case, a purple object (50C 50M) is being placed against a light yellow (60Y) background, so the lighter background must trap to the darker object.

2. Select the line art. Select Stroke in the Paint Style dialog box.

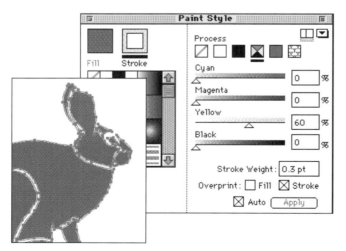

3. Make your stroke the same color as the tint that will surround the image, and an appropriate weight for printing conditions.

4. Select Overprint so that the stroke will provide a trap by overprinting the background tint color in the page layout program (see page 87, fig. 3).

How to trap type

Readability is the first concern regarding text (assuming that you want it read). Once this is established, secondary concerns like trapping come into play.

Color and readability are closely related. For example: white or yellow type in a black background is highly readable. Red type in a black background is almost illegible.

If white type/black background is chosen, then trapping must be done accordingly for CMYK printing. Body text does not work well in multiple colors, nor does text under 12 points in size, composed of two or more colors. It is better to use a custom color (such as Pantone) for body text. Black text is the easiest to read and simplest to produce: it can simply overprint the other colors. If text is to use a color other than black, be sure that at least one solid (100%) ink is used (see page 87, fig. 2).

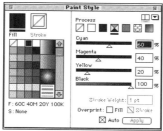

Using a draw program, create the desired text box, colored process black. To the white text inside the box, apply a white fill and a stroke of .3 points colored .1% cyan, .1% magenta, .1% yellow, and 100% black, set to Overprint. Stroke the outside of the box with the same settings.

You should now have a trapped text box. In this example, you are actually trapping the box to the paper color, white.

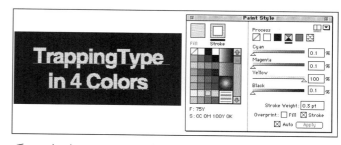

To apply the same procedure to yellow text, use these settings: .1% cyan, .1% magenta, 100% yellow, and .1% black.

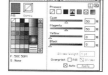

Outline type poses a special trapping problem: the border line around the type may not allow enough room to trap the background colors beneath it. Outline type should be used only if the outlines are thick enough to allow the overlapping of adjacent colors, or to allow the use of "bridge" colors. You will need to trap the characters' strokes by copying the the text, pasting it behind, and stroking it with an overprint value that exceeds the stroke in front by the required trapping value. Make the color of the background the predominant color.

Improperly trapped type can cause very expensive mistakes. Experiment before the job goes on press. One way to do this is to place trapping samples in the cut-off margins of a print job. You will see the actual results on press, without risk, and apply what you learn to the next job.

Proofs & Press Checks
Working with proofs

Using color proofs

Color proofs, in ascending order of accuracy and expense:

1. Desktop-generated proofs; i.e., laser, ink jet, bubblejet, computer/copier interface (such as a Canon/Fiery printout).

2. Desktop/Imagesetter proofs; Rainbow, Iris.

3. Film-generated (contact) proofs: Cromalin, Matchprint, color key, Dylux, black line.

4. Press proofs.

Loupes (or linen testers) come in a variety of shapes. A minimum of 6x magnification is necessary.

Electronically generated prepress proofs often cannot show trapping problems. Study the proof carefully with a loupe; you may be able to spot areas where there is not enough color overlap, and white lines are beginning to appear between colors. If these show up, some additional trapping work should be done on the system.

Use each level of proof as a guide when checking the next higher one:

Laser proofs: Check at this stage for copy corrections, type corrections, position and appearance (bitmapping) of graphics and photos, pagination, dimensions. Proofread several times. Changes made at this stage are the least costly.

Color laser or inkjet proofs: Check for general color placement, not accuracy.

Prefilm proofs (Iris, Rainbow, other proprietary brands): The most accurate proofs possible before film is output; sometimes used instead of film-generated proofs. Some can be printed on the paper stock to be used on press. Should give an accurate color representation, except for spot colors.

Film-generated proofs: A Dylux (blue-line) proof is a composite of all color plates in one pale blue image. Use this proof as a master to check all other film-generated proofs against for correct dimensions, pagination, graphics, fonts, text wrapping. Check also for "cleans" (extraneous marks) and broken type or rules. Mark corrections on the proof with a grease pencil or marker.

Color-key proofs: Used mainly for two-and three-color jobs to show color breaks, varnishes, and screens. Not an accurate rendering of color.

Cromalin, Matchprint, Pressmatch, etc.: Layers of color laminated in a glossy matrix; highly accurate. These are industry-standard contract proofs, the proofs used by printer and client as the agreed-upon proof to match for color on press.

How to check color separation proofs

Make sure that:

❖ All necessary printer's marks appear on all pages: file name, date, crop marks, registration marks.

❖ All graphic elements appear in correct position and fit properly.

❖ No pixellation appears in bitmap images; graphics look "clean."

❖ Bleeds extend the proper distance outside trim marks.

❖ Knockouts and overprints appear correct and in register.

- Trapping is done properly; there are no dropouts and no show-through.
- No moiré patterns appear.
- No banding appears in gradient fills.
- Pictures fit properly in frames with no gaps.
- CMYK colors look as expected; spot colors are in proper positions with no gaps. (Most proofing systems will not reproduce spot colors with total accuracy; attach a swatch to the proof for pressroom reference.)
- All text prints correctly without broken type or lines.
- No scratches, smudges, or spots appear.

Mark all questionable areas, no matter how slight, and call them to the printer/separator's attention. If the job is not perfect now, it will not improve on press.

If you need to reoutput a separation, have all plates for the page output at the same time to ensure accurate registration.

How to do a press OK

Bring your prepress proof with you to the press check and use it as a guide for you and the pressman.

A press session begins with makeready (setting up plates, paper, and press tests); then a few sample sheets are printed for examination. These are press proofs; you will see the actual effect of the ink on the chosen paper. This is the last chance to make adjustments. Minor problems, such as color balance, may be fixable at this point by the pressman.

Check the sample pages carefully, using the same criteria you used when checking prepress proofs. Pay particular attention to critical colors like flesh tones. Make sure everything looks in register; look at the edges of square halftones and multicolor tints (you may want to use a loupe). If a color crosses a gutter, check both pages to make sure they match. Check page breaks and folio numbers for correct order; fold up a page signature to check the imposition (the order of the pages.) Request that a dummy book be made up for your examination.

Mark anything that looks wrong with a grease pencil or marker. You will be shown progressive proofs (progs) as press adjustments are made to address any problems noted.

When you are satisfied with everything about the page or form (group of imposed pages) being printed, initial it, noting the time and date with your OK. Request a few press proofs to take for future reference.

Photo & Image Processing
Working with large image files

High-resolution 24-bit color images are memory hogs, and they must be decompressed for editing work. Along with increasing available RAM, there are a few other fixes that enable you to handle large image files.

How to use virtual memory

Virtual memory is the use of extra hard disk space to create a sort of auxiliary RAM.

Check your computer's control panels for a switch to turn virtual memory on and off and to set the amount (up to twice the amount of RAM in your computer). If you are using an image-editing program, it may have a built-in device for accessing hard disk space for virtual memory. This method works more slowly than using actual RAM, but it will at least allow you to work.

If you have several hard disks, you can designate the one with the most free space as the scratch disk for image editing, thus taking advantage of virtual memory. It is best to do this with a non-removable drive. This is another good reason to install a spacious extra drive!

How to use Photoshop's Quick Edit to manage a large image file

If you need to edit a large bitmap file and you are short on RAM, try using this exceptionally useful Photoshop feature.

Open your original image file, save and rename it as a new file in one of these formats: Photoshop 2.0, Scitex CT, or uncompressed TIFF. Close the original file, and choose Acquire-Quick Edit from the Photoshop File menu. In the dialog box, open the new file you just created. It will appear as a thumbnail in a selection window. Use the Marquee tool or adjust the built-in grid to choose a small area of the large file to edit. The much smaller file size of the area you've chosen will be displayed in megabytes. Click OK. Now, instead of poking through a 50 MB file edit, you can quickly edit a small area of that file. When the edit is finished, choose Export-Quick Edit from the File menu. Your edit will be saved to the new image file. Repeat the process on all the areas you want to change. If you need to make a global change to the image, you need to open the entire file. When finished, resave the file in whatever format you need for display and output.

How to make smaller Photoshop files

When saving a final CMYK Photoshop file in EPS format, you can reduce the size of the file by 10 to 400% by using JPEG compression encoding. (Not all imagesetters or systems can handle JPEG: check with the output destination before using this option.) Specify this option in the EPS Save dialog box. The Maximum Quality setting offers significant compression, with no perceptible loss of image quality when output from a PostScript Level 2 device.

You can then resave the image for FPO use, in 72 ppi resolution, producing an extremely small file for placement in a page layout. The resolution of most monitors, 72 ppi, is adequate for on-screen work and low-resolution printouts.

Caution: If you anticipate the need to edit the file further, save an uncompressed version, too. Continually resaving in JPEG format can eventually degrade image quality to unacceptable levels.

How to correct photo images in Photoshop

Steps for digital image processing

1. Monitor calibration: to be sure that what you see is what you get.

2. Scanning at correct input resolution: for file size, reproduction size, and output device resolution.

3. Color correction: for optimal tonal values, color hues, brightness, and contrast.

4. Channel modification: to control pixel noise.

5. Special effects: silhouetting, glows, drop shadows, and filter effects for further enhancement or creative alteration.

6. Unsharp masking: to bring out maximum image sharpness.

In general, rescan rather than correcting. All color correction removes some data. If your original photo looked fine but the scanned image looks bad, the scanner is at fault: try rescanning with adjusted settings. High-end scanners offer far more control at this stage, and should be considered for color-critical images.

If the original photo is the problem, evaluate the image and plan your approach. Low-contrast or muddy images usually lack the entire tonal range available, from white to black. Scan at the proper resolution, trying to correct as many exposure and color balance problems as possible in the scanning process. Crop the image to the area you need. Adjust the gamma (exposure), setting the white and black points (lightest highlights and darkest shadows). For many images, these steps may be sufficient.

To adjust the white and black points

Use the Levels command from the Image/Adjust menu. You can make adjustments by dragging the black and white sliders, or by sampling the lightest or darkest areas from the image and setting these to pure white or black. Move the eyedropper/cursor over the image and select the lightest area. Click on the white eyedropper in the Levels dialog box,

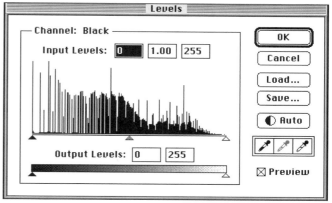

redefining your selection as pure white and adjusting all other colors accordingly. Do the same for the black point. This should greatly improve the image. Bear in mind that 100% white or black in halftones can produce problems on press, appearing as washed-out highlights or muddy shadows. Therefore, use the output slider to set the white point at 250 (3% dot) and the black point at 6 (98% dot).

To fine-tune overall exposure, use the central gray slider in the Levels box to adjust the midtones. When you are satisfied, click OK to apply your corrections. You can save these settings to use later, too.

Other tools to try are the Brightness/Contrast settings and Variations. These are less exact, but can be good for quick fixes.

Color correction

Photoshop's Levels and Curves make it possible to check an image's highlights, midtones, and shadows and make adjustments to balance color and tonality while retaining detail (see page 87, fig.4). The Histogram and Densitometer (in the Info window) permit you to check color values and make corrections. Hue and Saturation, Color Balance, and Selective Color may be adjusted as final correction steps. Do the modifications at 1:1 zoom ratio.

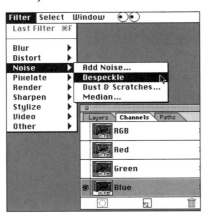

Channel color modification

A grayscale image has one channel (black); RGB has three (red, green, blue); and CMYK has four (cyan, magenta, yellow, black). Each channel stores information about its respective color. By inspecting an image's channels individually, you can see if modification is needed.

The RGB blue channel is usually the most coarse or grainy, due to pixel noise from the scanner. Using the Despeckle filter on this or a combination of channels can reduce the graininess.

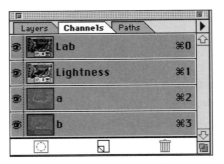

Conversion of an RGB image to LAB color mode offers another method of channel modification. The LAB mode contains three channels: Lightness, A (green to red), and B (blue to yellow). The Blue channel may benefit from the Despeckling filter or from the Dust and Scratch filter, to combat extreme noise. The Lightness channel can be unsharp-masked, lightened, and darkened without affecting color hues.

Any of Photoshop's effects may be applied to selected areas of an image. The best way to make the selection is with the vector Pen tool, which offers the most precision. Using the Lasso tool in conjunction with the Option key is a quick-selection alternative, but less accurate.

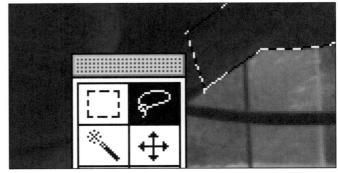

Enhancing detail in photo images

"Unsharp masking" is derived from a printer's term for sharpening an image for use on press. Most scanned images can benefit from this procedure. Generally, the higher the quality of the digital image, the greater the percentage it can be sharpened. Unsharp masking (to accentuate tonal changes) and Smoothing (for large color or tonal areas) can be used together or selectively. Unsharp masking can spark up a lackluster photo and make details stand out by accentuating contrast in areas where light and dark meet. Anticipate this when measuring highlight and shadow values during tonal and color correction: allow a little flexibility in the tonal range.

You can also apply this filter selectively to detail areas and color channels with no visible film grain.

Burn and Dodge tools can sharpen an image by subtly bringing out details in otherwise washed-out or muddy areas.

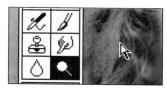

This old photo was badly faded before it was scanned and retouched with Photoshop's Burn and Dodge tools. Note the restored detail in the face, hair, and lace (see page 87, fig. 7).

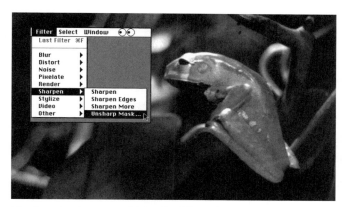

Viewing the image at 1:1 in the Filter dialog box, make adjustments according to this formula:

Amount = intensity of effect; Radius = width of edge definition; Threshold = film grain detection

Start with these settings:

Amount: 200% , Radius: 1.5 pixels, Threshold: 5 levels.

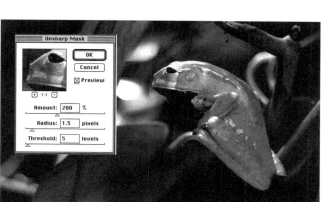

Observe the subtle improvements of definition in detail areas and transitions from light to dark areas (see page 87, fig. 5).

How to clean up a badly damaged photo

Badly flawed areas on old photos can be repaired with Photoshop's Dust and Scratches filter. Try selecting a scratched area with a slight feather added to the selection marquee (to soften the edge of the selection). Give the selection enough area for the filter to draw from, but not large enough to blot out important details.

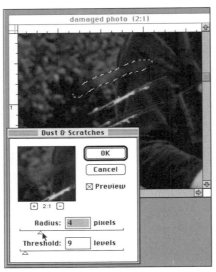

Choose the Dust and Scratches Filter; set a low Radius and a high Threshold. Adjust the Threshold setting gradually, with the Preview option activated. When the blemish begins to fade, raise the Radius setting until the flaw is gone. If some damage still remains, use the Smudge tool set at a low to medium percentage, and blend the flawed area into its surroundings.

For larger damaged areas, use the above technique, then switch to the Rubber Stamp tool to clone unflawed areas into the damaged part.

The retouched photo

Converting a color photo to black-and-white

When you are given a color photo to work with and you need a black-and-white image for publication, use image-editing software to convert the color image to grayscale. Scan the photo as a 24-bit color image, optimizing it for its full range of hues and tones. Once you are satisfied with the color image, use the Mode command to convert to grayscale. This way, you retain all the tonal values of the original. You can now adjust the black-and-white image as needed (see page 87, fig. 6).

Working with duotones and tints

How to convert a photo to a duotone

In an image-editing pro-gram, open a grayscale image (or a color image converted to grayscale). Choose the Duotone command. The default first color will be black. You may want to adjust default settings to conform to output requirements (check with your printer). Choose a second color, generally lighter than the first. Adjust the duotone curves to obtain the rela-tive intensity and contrast you want. Slightly different curve settings can produce dramatically different results. If necessary, make adjustments in the levels. You may want to save the final setting for use on other photos. Save the image as an EPS.

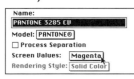

Change the screen angle of an imported duotone's second (lighter) color to 70% (the magenta angle) in your page layout program, so that one ink will not cover the other when printed. For tritones or more inks, ask your printer for the correct angles.

You can create a simple duotone effect by placing a light tint behind a TIFF image. Another approach is to sandwich TIFFs, colorizing one and adjusting its ink screen angle (see page 88, figs. 1 and 2).

To create two spot-color tints

Sandwich two picture or text boxes, and fill each box with the color and percentage of ink required for the tint you want. Then set the lighter of the inks to Overprint. You may need to adjust the screen angle for that ink as well.

Combining a duotone with a black-and-white image

Open a grayscale image in an image-editing program. Resave it as a separate file for the duotone portion. Select the area you want to use as a duotone by creating a path around it and save the path as a clipping path. Convert the image to a duo-tone and save as an EPS. You can now superimpose the duotone image on the grayscale image in a draw-ing or page layout program (see page 88, fig. 3).

Working with clipping paths

In order to have a bitmap image "knock out" of a background, the image must have a clipping path around its edge.

To create a clipping path, open the image in an image-editing program. Using the Pen tool (or any Path tool), draw an outline around an area of the image. It is best not to use a selection tool like Photoshop's Magic Wand to create a path, since this produces too many control points, a potential output problem. If you want to have "holes" in the image, you can simply draw paths around those areas and make them part of the outline path; the areas will become transparent. Once the path is completed, save it as a clipping path. Leave the flatness setting blank; the output device determines the correct value. (If you save the file with a flatness value, specify at least three pixels.) You do not need to remove the background; only the area within the clipping path will display or print out when the image is imported.

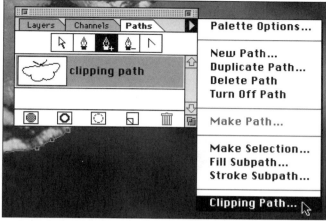

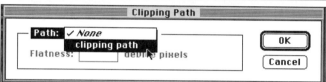

Page layout programs handle clipping paths differently. Pagemaker can import clipping paths with both EPS and TIFF images; Quark will accept only the EPS clipping path format.

When you want a text runaround with a clipping-path image, let the shape of the image's picture box create the runaround, rather than using an "auto image" option. This gives better control of text flow (see page 88, fig. 4).

Selectively applying a filter to a bitmap image

1. Create a shape for the filter effect in a draw program. Open the bitmap image in an image-editing program, and also open the shape from the draw program.

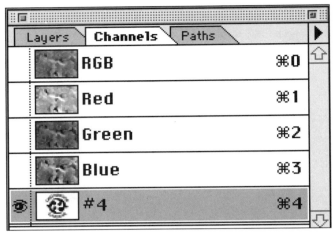

2. Choose Select All/Copy. Create a new channel in the image file; select Paste.

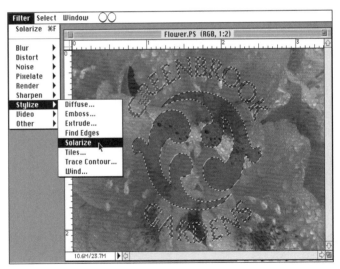

3. Return to the main image channel and choose Load Selection. If you wish to affect the opposite area of the image, choose Inverse Selection also. Apply any filter or combination of filters for the desired effect.

Here, the Solarization filter was applied to the channel selection (see page 88, fig. 5).

Scanning & Resolution
Resolution

A bitmap image requiring editing or color correction, or destined for print, needs to have sufficiently high resolution for output. That resolution will depend on the reproduction size of the image, the output device, and the final line screen to be used.

When ordering a high-resolution scan, you can specify the format in which you want the files to be saved, and have them returned to you on a CD for convenient archiving.

How to determine image resolution

To use a bitmapped image successfully, it must have the correct resolution. Otherwise, it will be jagged or pixellated when it is output. Unlike vector-created PostScript images (which have almost infinite scalability), bitmaps are limited in how much they can be resized without loss of quality; the resolution is finite.

Three interdependent resolution numbers come into play with a bitmapped image:

1. Scan resolution, measured in dpi (dots per inch) or, more correctly, ppi (pixels per inch). This determines the amount of image information (pixels) stored in the image file. This resolution is controlled by the settings in the software that drives the scanner. Example: a black-and-white line drawing scanned at 300 dpi, to be reproduced at the scanned size.

200% enlargement of a vector image…

…and a bitmapped image. Note pixellation.

This also applies to bitmap images generated in paint or image-editing applications.

2. Halftone resolution, measured in lpi (lines per inch). This is a term from the world of offset lithography, denoting the resolution with which the tonal values in a continuous-tone image, such as a photo, can be reproduced in print. For example, 85 lpi is the standard resolution for most newspaper photos.

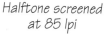

Halftone screened at 85 lpi

Halftone screened at 150 lpi

3. Output resolution, measured in dpi, which expresses the capability of the printer or output device to reproduce detail. Example: a high-resolution imagesetter producing an output of 2,540 dpi, compared to a lower-resolution 300 dpi laser printer.

There is also a designation for other image usages, such as on-screen or online, generally measured in ppi. The resolution generally used for on-screen images is 72 ppi, the resolution of most monitors.

Two formulas to determine the correct resolution for a printed image

The first formula estimates the number of pixels needed in both dimensions of the image:

Line screen (lpi) x printed image dimension x 2 = minimum image dimension (ppi)
Example:
150 lpi x 2.5″ high x 2 = 750 pixels high
150 lpi x 2″ wide x 2 = 600 pixels wide

The second formula is useful when the image will be reduced or enlarged from its original size and gives the required final resolution in dpi:

Reproduction size (%) x line screen (lpi) x 2 = required image resolution (dpi)
Example:
150% x 150 lpi x 2 = 450 dpi

Although a bitmap image should be either scanned or resampled and saved in the correct resolution for each size used, there is another way to match the image size to the resolution of the output device. Use this formula to figure out the right resizing base multiple:

Image resolution (dpi) ÷ printer resolution (dpi) X 100 = resizing base percent

Examples:
72 dpi (bitmap image) ÷ 300 dpi (laser printer) X 100 = 24%
Scale the bitmap image by any whole-number multiple of 24%: 48, 72, 96, etc.

For a high-resolution imagesetter (1,270–2,540 dpi), use as a base scaling value a multiple of 17%: 34, 51, 68, 85, 102, etc.

Resampling an image (changing the dpi and size using software) will always compromise the quality of the image by reducing detail. It should be done only when absolutely necessary.

Line art

Line art often requires a higher resolution than halftones, to prevent jagged edges (halftones tend to mask them). For fine line art, 600 dpi is good; 800 to 1,000 dpi is optimal.

Line art scanned at 300 dpi

Line art scanned at 600 dpi

Scanning a three-dimensional object

This technique is handy for package design, product catalogs, and comping.

First, decide whether you want a light or a dark background, based on the object you want to scan and how the scan is to be used. Place the object on your flatbed scanner. Then drape an opaque fabric over it. For a light background, white felt works well; for a dark background, use black velveteen. When scanning, try several prescan settings to adjust exposure and compensate for reflections; you may need to make several scans to get it right. You can then process the image, trace it as a template, or use it as-is.

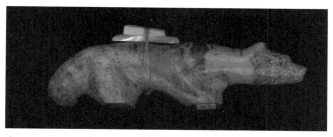

Image scanned against black velvet background

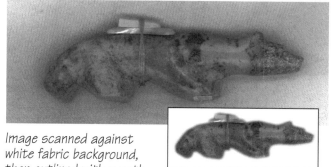

Image scanned against white fabric background, then outlined with a path and selected. The selection was then feathered and inverted, and the background was deleted.

For an interesting collage effect, arrange various objects on the scanner and drape with a textured fabric background; then scan as described above.

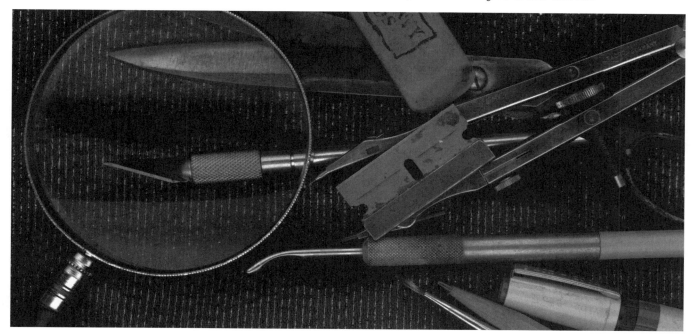

Scanning tips

How to position art on a flatbed scanner

Square top edge with T-square and knife

You can save cleanup time by making sure that the image you scan is squared up. To do this, use a T-square to find the image's horizontal, and tape the paper containing the image to your drawing board. Cut the top of the paper off using the T-square. You can now position the art on the scanner's bed with the squared-off top flush to the raised lip of the scanning bed.

If the art to be scanned is too close to the top of the paper, use a spacer cut from white cover stock to position the art lower on the scanning bed.

If you have to scan some art or a photo that is hard to locate in your scanner's preview, use one of these tricks to isolate the area to be scanned:

For small images, such as frames on a photo contact sheet, isolate the area to scan with a frame of white drafting tape or post-it notes.

For a larger image, cut two L-shaped pieces of black card stock and use them to frame the area, taping them in place. You can then quickly pinpoint the area to scan.

Testing your scanner

To locate the place on your scanner's bed where art is most faithfully converted to a scan, scan a sheet of opaque white cover stock at a low resolution. In an image-editing program, use the Equalize command on the scan file. You will see, on your monitor, any flaws in the scanner's path, and can then avoid placing critical art in those areas.

Tracing with Streamline

For fine line work, do your drawing at 200% and scan it full size, then trace it. Set the noise level at zero in the Conversion Options to improve accuracy. You can reduce the finished art by 50%, to reproduction size, in your draw program.

Scanning halftone images

Screened original

When you scan a photo that has already been screened to a halftone (for example, a printed image), you also get the dot pattern in your scan. This can cause problems later, when the scanned image is rescreened for output, producing moiré patterns or other undesired results.

Rescreened scan

Normal halftone pattern, magnified

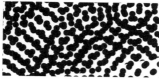

Moiré pattern in rescreened halftone, magnified

Here are two ways to counteract this problem:

1. Scan the original at your scanner's highest resolution to record the maximum amount of information; the moiré-fixing process will discard some image detail. After bringing the image into Photoshop, zoom in so you can see the halftone dot (or noise) pattern in the scanned image.

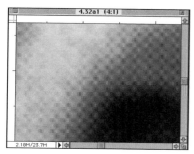

Closeup of a scanned halftone, showing the dot pattern in the grayscale image.

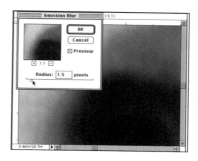

Choose the Gaussian Blur filter, and blur the image just enough to merge the individual dots into each other. Zoom back out to check the effect on the whole image; if too much quality was sacrificed, try a lower setting. Adjust the tonal balance in the Levels or Curves dialog boxes to bring out contrast. Choose the Unsharp Mask filter, using the same Radius value previously used in the Gaussian Blur. Get the image as sharp as possible to compensate for the blurring. When you are satisfied, sample the image down to its final size and resolution.

Some scanners have built-in capabilities to deal with moiré patterns.

2. Scan the image at the size and resolution you will need for final output. Then bring the image into an image-editing application and use the Despeckle filter to "blend" the dots in the halftone pattern into the surrounding pixels. A Blur filter, used selectively, can help, too.

If the dot pattern is really coarse or pronounced, consider converting the photo to line art, possibly even accentuating the halftone screen!

Corrected image

A makeshift transparency scanner

Most desktop flatbed scanner manufacturers sell add-on transparency modules for scanning 35 mm, 4" x 5", or larger photos. Despite manufacturer claims, the value of these costly add-ons is questionable. Unless the volume of your work warrants the purchase of a high-end scanning system, you are probably better off sending out to a trade shop for high-resolution transparency scans. You might also consider having the images saved in photo CD form, depending on their intended use.

For low-resolution FPO use, you can rig up a simple transparency module for your flatbed scanner with a small portable light box.

To scan a 4" x 5" or larger image, just tape it to the lightbox and place the box upside down on the scanner's bed. Do a preview scan and adjust the scanner's setting for the sharpest image you can get, then scan.

A portable light box is a widely available, inexpensive, and versatile tool for examining photo transparencies and film, tracing artwork, checking proofs, and many other studio tasks. It can be very useful for displaying transparencies in a client's office, too.

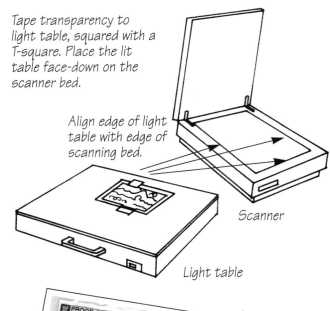

Tape transparency to light table, squared with a T-square. Place the lit table face-down on the scanner bed.

Align edge of light table with edge of scanning bed.

Scanner

Light table

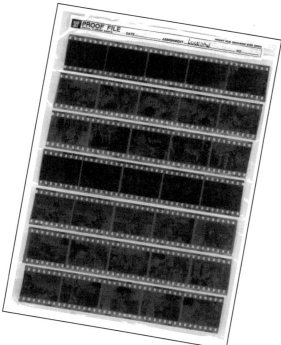

Load 35 mm transparencies or negatives into a clear plastic sleeve (available at photo supply stores), tape to the light box, and scan.

Hardware & Software Tips
Floppy disk tips

A floppy disk ejects automatically from a Mac upon shutdown or when its icon is dragged to the trash. Using the Eject command from the Special menu leaves a ghost icon on the desktop. The command is really useful only when you want to copy one disk to another or as a first resort when the disk won't eject another way.

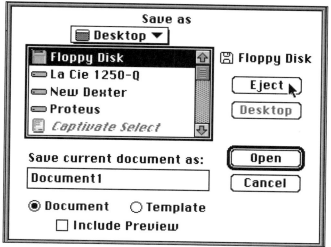

To eject a disk while you are still in an application, select Save As from the File menu. Click Drive if the name of the disk does not appear in the dialog box. Click Eject. Click Cancel to return to the application.

To eject a floppy from an internal drive, press Command/Shift/1.

When you send a supplier critical files for output, use new disks and lock them.

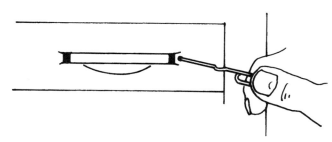

To eject a stuck floppy disk from a Mac, push the straight end of an unbent paper clip into the small hole to the right of the floppy drive opening. Give a quick, firm push (not a jab) when you feel resistance; the disk should pop out. Keep that paper clip handy, but use it only when all else fails! If you still encounter difficulty, the disk's label may be partly peeled off, and hung up in the drive. Using the above maneuver, keep the paper clip pushed in and the floppy at eject level, and very gently try to ease it out with needlenose pliers.

Always reboot after using this technique.

How to clean a mouse

If your cursor starts moving erratically when you move your mouse, it's a good bet that the mouse's inner works have gotten gummed up with debris collected over time from the mouse pad or desk. Fabric mouse pads are especially prone to deposit fine fibers inside the trackball area. Here's how to clean up:

1. Shut down the computer and unplug the mouse cable.

2. Turn the plastic ring on the mouse's underside counterclockwise. Holding your hand over the ring, turn the mouse over; the ring and ball will fall out into your hand.

3. Dip a cotton swab in rubbing alcohol and gently scrub the little rollers around the ball's housing, and the ball cage itself. If there are some fibers stuck in the wheel assembly, you may need to work them out with a pair of small tweezers. Set the mouse aside to dry.

4. Clean the ball by washing it with tap water and detergent; rinse well and dry completely with a lint-free cloth.

5. Replace the ball and ring, tightening the ring until it locks.

6. Plug in the mouse and restart the computer. Your mouse should now roll smoothly.

This also works on trackballs. For other input devices, check the manual.

A dirty keyboard can be cleaned with a soft cloth dampened with all-purpose household spray cleaner or denatured alcohol. To clean the inside, try a vacuum cleaner with a soft brush attatchment, or a blast of canned freon, available from a photo supply store.

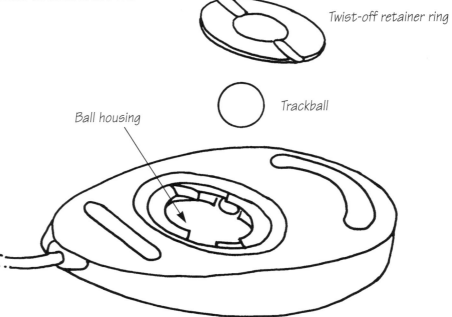

Twist-off retainer ring

Trackball

Ball housing

Buying equipment

CPU speeds double about every one to two years; the price of memory decreases by half over roughly the same time span. Software companies issue major upgrades every few years, and minor upgrades almost weekly. Correspondingly, standards and expectations change at the same rate. It is almost impossible to stay current, so relax. When planning a purchase, use the one-to-two-year mark as a guide.

Before shopping, assess your future needs. What sort of work will you be doing? What types of software will you use, and what are the system requirements? As a rule of thumb, buy the fastest drives, the most memory, and the highest resolution that you can afford. With the computer itself, look for upgradability so it can grow with your needs. Study product reviews in magazines, and get literature from manufacturers by mail, fax, or at their web sites. Most important, ask your colleagues what they use or plan to purchase.

Buying hardware

Should you mail-order direct from the manufacturer or from one of the companies who advertise in magazines, or buy from a local reseller? The choice is basically a trade-off between convenience, pricing, security, and added values.

Mail order

Advantages: Shop from home, competitive prices (expect 40–50% below list for software, around 40% below list for some hardware), quick-to-research prices, avoid sales taxes with out-of-state vendors, home delivery.

Disadvantages: Can't pretest or examine product, no local support. Some vendors are lax at best in their customer service; some are downright unscrupulous. Getting satisfaction in such cases can be very frustrating.

If you consider mail order, protect yourself:

❖ Check with colleagues to see if they have experience with the vendor.

❖ When you call the vendor, ask the sales rep how long the company has been in business. Is it an authorized reseller for the product you want to purchase? Specify the model number for hardware, version number for software; list all parts and add-ons you expect (such as cables, ink cartridges, etc.) and confirm that they are included.

❖ Confirm warranties and compatibility; state which platform you're using.

❖ Be clear about the terms of the purchase. Is the product available now, or is it back-ordered? Will you accept a substitute in case the product you want is unavailable? Substitutions cannot be made without your consent. Have the salesperson repeat your order, and all terms, to you for confirmation. Have the order faxed to you.

❖ Ask what additional parts are needed, and their availability. You want to make sure you have everything you need to get up and running. For example, many printers and monitors require special adapters for connection to a Mac system.

❖ Ask if the hardware is new or used ("reconditioned") and state whether a reconditioned product is acceptable. Reconditioned units can offer good functionality at a bargain price, but do entail some risk. Find out the circumstances of the reconditioning: who did it, and why. Was it a manufacturer's factory job?

❖ Buy only from a company that offers a no-questions-asked, 30-day money-back guarantee. If the vendor doesn't offer this, look elsewhere. Find out the procedure for making a return: is a return authorization number necessary? How would it be obtained? What is the policy in general, and in regard to your product specifically? Ask if the salesperson has the power to authorize a return and refund. If not, find out the name of the person who can. If you get vague answers or non-cooperation, look elsewhere.

❖ Ask about technical support, which would ideally come from the vendor. This is generally the case in purchases direct from the manufacturer. If the vendor doesn't provide this service, find out if the original manufacturer will provide support for a product purchased from this vendor.

❖ Get a commitment on the product's delivery date. All mail-order purchases are supposed to be shipped within 30 days, according to the Uniform Commercial Code. If you need the product by a certain date, specify this, and ask about shipping options and prices.

❖ Make sure that the vendor is responsible for all shipping and tracking of the product. Ask who pays shipping costs for returns (usually, it's the buyer).

❖ Always pay with a credit card; never send cash, check, or money order. The credit card can help to protect you from fraud, and gives you another recourse if the vendor does not honor its part of the transaction.

❖ Make a paper trail: it will help in the event of a dispute. Write down your conversation with the vendor's salesperson, including that person's name, the date and time of your call, all information given on the product, and all terms, warranty, shipping, and policy information. Keep all paperwork pertaining to the transaction, including shipping documents. Keep a copy of the vendor's ad or catalog, too.

❖ Know whom to contact in case of an unresolved dispute. Some resources:

Your credit card company

The magazine carrying the vendor's ad

The Better Business Bureau in the vendor's state

The Attorney General's office in the vendor's state

The consumer protection agency in your state

The U.S. Postal Service

Local reseller

Advantages: Can test products on-site, establish a personal relationship, local tech support and service, installation support, easy returns.

Disadvantages: Probably higher prices. Always expect to pay more for personal service and knowledgeable guidance.

Ask a retailer the same questions you would ask of a mail-order vendor. When making a major purchase, such as a computer system, monitor, or printer, it could well be worth sacrificing some price discounts for the peace of mind of having support close by. You may also want to ask about having your equipment installed, which may involve a short training session. Discuss maintenance contracts; they can be worthy investments.

Choosing and buying software

The same caveats and advice for buying hardware also apply to software. Doing your homework is doubly important, because software is more difficult to return if it proves inadequate to your needs. If possible, "test-drive" the application before you buy. Trade shows and weekend classes are great places to do this; you get to try out new hardware, too. Make sure you purchase the latest version, and that the manufacturer is not poised to release a major upgrade any day soon. Make sure you're getting the full version, and not a beta (test) or LE (limited capabilities) copy. Be aware that some hardware comes bundled with software you may want (many scanners ship with the full version of Photoshop and an OCR application) and plan purchases accordingly.

Don't forget about shareware and freeware, available through user groups, online sources, and publications. Remember to reimburse shareware developers whose products you use; suggested amounts and addresses are usually documented in the software.

Do your homework online

The Internet, a wonderful tool for communicating with your customers and colleagues, is also an invaluable resource for researching and purchasing equipment and software.

A search with a web browser will produce web sites for suppliers whose products you are considering. You can get current information, post questions to customer-service e-mail addresses, find local resellers, and place orders for most software. You can download fonts, clip art, photo images, and many other graphic products.

Get a Guru

A competent computer consultant who is familiar with electronic publishing is an indispensable ally. When you form a professional relationship with a guru, you are benefitting from his or her exposure to current trends, tools, and techniques. This gives you valuable knowledge, with which to make planning and buying decisions.

Search for a consultant as you would for any service provider. Solicit referrals from associates and user groups. Interview prospective consultants, stating your needs and describing the nature of your business and creative goals. Ask about hourly rates and other billing options. What areas of expertise does the consultant possess? Check references.

Regard your chosen computer guru as a teacher as well as a troubleshooter; you want to be able to handle minor problems on your own, and he or she can show you how. View your consultant's fee as an investment in your business and in your own knowledge base.

Surge suppression and data protection

Even with regular backup (which is essential), a power surge or brownout can fry circuitry or cause data loss in computers and peripherals. If you are a single user working in an area with reliable power, extra protection may be unnecessary. Internal surge suppression in Macintosh computers and peripherals is excellent. However, if you work in an area prone to lightning strikes or power shortages (such as a rural area or an inadequately powered work space), external protection is a good idea. Two basic types are available.

Surge Suppressors

A surge suppressor, often built into a power strip, protects hardware from high-voltage surges. This is the least costly form of protection, but it does not necessarily protect data. Cheaper models function like fuses, blowing up to save equipment further down the power line. More advanced suppressors can survive large power spikes while delivering safe power to the computer. They can also offer superior filtration of electronic noise, which can come from other devices in the same circuit (such as a coffee pot). A good additional feature is the ability to protect equipment connected by network cabling and phone lines. The lowest-cost (and ultimately the safest) alternative is to unplug your computer and peripherals from wall sockets and phone jacks when a thunderstorm blows in or when equipment is unattended. Ideally, your computer and peripherals should be on their own circuit, thus avoiding further power drain and noise.

Uninterruptable Power Supply

A UPS is the next level of protection, offering the same safeguards as a surge suppressor, with the additional advantage of supplying backup power for a long-enough period to allow equipment to be shut down in a power outage, thus saving precious data. It may also be possible to run equipment from the UPS's backup power supply, long enough to complete a work session. The higher degree of protection carries a correspondingly higher price tag. Two types are available. A standby UPS passes AC power from outlet to computer, switching over to an internal battery when a power failure occurs. An inverter changes the DC current to AC, for the computer's use.

An online UPS, the highest (and costliest) degree of protection, constantly routes power from outlet to computer through a DC power supply, which also functions as a battery charger. In a power outage, power is drawn immediately from the battery. The unit constantly monitors power consistency, and adjusts as necessary, making it ideal for areas with chronic power fluctuations. A budget alternative is the regulating standby UPS, which uses a transformer to smooth out power fluctuations. Some UPS units can initiate automatic shutdown for an unattended system.

A caveat: do not connect your laser printer to a UPS backup; it will discharge the battery very quickly. Put it on a surge suppressor, instead.

Evaluate your needs for protection

❖ What is the impact of your geographic area and physical environment on power reliability?

❖ What is your work situation? A standby unit is probably sufficient protection for a single user; a network could warrant a UPS.

❖ What level of protection can you afford (or afford not to have)?

❖ How many outlets do you need?

❖ Can the unit self-monitor its battery charge?

❖ What is the VA rating (in the case of a UPS)? The unit needs to be matched to your system's requirements. Here's the formula:

Add up the power requirements (volt-amps) of all equipment that will draw power from the UPS. To determine the VAs, check the back of the equipment for amperes required, total, and multiply by 120. For equipment rated in watts, divide the total watts required by .7 to get the VAs.

Other protection issues and devices

Business insurance is an important form of protection to include in your arsenal. Talk to your agent about computer, peripheral, and software coverage (most renter's and home-owner's policies can have riders attached). Consider insurance for business interruption and loss of records and data, too. Don't forget yourself: investigate disability insurance. Your machines won't earn a living if you can't run them.

Install and use a virus protection program (such as SAM) on your computer. Virus protection is especially important on a PC, which is subject to a greater number of hostile viruses than a Mac.

Memory and CPU tips

RAM

Your applications each need a certain amount of dedicated RAM to run smoothly. Large files may need even more RAM to process. If you are getting Out of Memory error messages, try increasing the memory allotted to that application (on a Mac, open the program's Get Info box and type in a higher minimum memory amount). Quitting other applications while you work on a large file should help, too.

The price of additional RAM chips fluctuates continually. Check the display ads in the back of computer magazines and call around for the best price. Installing new memory is a simple process; the chips usually come with installation instructions (ask before you buy). If you don't feel comfortable attempting installation yourself, shop for a dealer, service shop, or freelance technician who can do it for you (on site, if possible).

In addition to RAM, you may need to add more VRAM to power your monitor, especially if yours is over 17". VRAM controls the resolution and the number of colors available for display; the more VRAM, the more colors. For heavy image-editing work, you may want to add a graphics card (which is another form of memory for monitor display). They are pricey, but can speed up your editing work considerably, and carry other benefits such as increased/adjustable display resolutions.

On the Mac, basic functions such as Cut, Copy, and Paste are affected by a portion of memory called the system heap. As fonts, utilities, and other extensions are added, the system can choke up. To see if your system's heap is large enough for safe use, select About This Macintosh from the Apple menu. The bar graphs that appear show the amount of free space, which should be about 25% of the length of the system's bar. You can use a utility like CE Software's HeapFixer to allocate more memory at startup to the system heap. Start by adding 100K to the current size, as shown in the top of the dialog box, and restart the Mac. You may need to repeat this process two or three times until you have the right balance.

You can never have too much RAM, especially for image-editing tasks, which can require memory three to five times the size of the image file! Adding additional RAM is a good investment; it will speed your work and expand your computer's capabilities.

CPU tips

There are conflicting schools of thought on turning your computer off at night. The "pros" say shutting down saves some wear and tear due to heat buildup, and can save electricity, too. The "cons" say the surge of powering up causes wear and tear, too, and requires more power. It really comes down to personal preference and convenience. An energy-saving solution is to turn off your monitor and printer (both major power consumers) at day's end. It won't hurt your CPU to leave it on.

Many newer operating systems can put computers and monitors in a low-power standby mode, a good compromise which does not require a complete reboot.

One point in favor of keeping the computer on: you could run an automatic backup or file-copying program while you sleep!

Printer issues

PostScript

For doing serious graphic work, a PostScript printer is a requirement. Any PostScript printer with a serial port should work with either a PC or a Mac. Most printers are either configured for PostScript operation, or for an emulation mode (based on the HP Laserjet). The Mac's generic LaserWriter driver is a general-purpose PostScript driver that can drive most PostScript printers in the absence of the driver created for that printer, which should be available from the manufacturer, either in a disk or as a download from an online site. You need to select the appropriate driver in the Mac's Chooser for the printer you wish to use.

Your new printer may arrive without a connection cable; some printers also require adapters between connections to the computer. Ask about this when you purchase, stating the model of your computer. This way, your printer will be ready to connect and use when you unpack it.

When to check a Mac's Chooser settings

The Chooser dialog box displays the specific printers available for use.

❖ When you print for the first time from a new printer

❖ When you have a problem getting a document to print

❖ When you change from one printer to another

❖ When you want to send a file to another device than a printer, such as a modem, a plotter, or another computer on a network

❖ When you change the connections on your Mac or printer

❖ When you want to join an active network (select the Appletalk Zone section and be sure Appletalk is turned on)

Make sure that you select the icon of the printer you wish to use, the name of the printer in the scroll menu, and the appropriate PPD (software specific to the printer you are using,) when necessary, from the Setup dialog box.

When preparing a file in Persuasion or Powerpoint for slide imaging, make sure the Mac's Chooser is set for Laserwriter, not Laserwriter 8.0, QMS, or some other driver, or the image will be too big for 35 mm.

Printing cover-weight stock on a laser printer

Heavy stock can cause paper jams, especially when the paper has a rough texture. Three solutions are to switch to a non-textured cover stock, to burnish the leading edge of each page to flatten it, or to print out the text weight of that stock, then laminate it to a thicker sheet with spray cement.

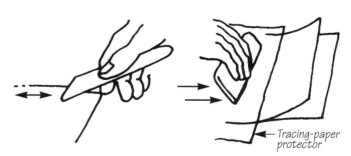

Compressing the edge of a cover stock sheet with a burnishing tool.

Laminating a spray-cemented text-weight sheet to a thicker sheet.

Print Error messages

```
Currently Processing:
Page: 2
[                                    ]

Picture: New Dexter:...:MU scans:Perky Patty w/card
[████████████              ]

To cancel printing,
hold down the ⌘ key and type a period (.)
```

Error messages are often caused by memory problems. If you get a PostScript error message while
printing a Quark file, you can track down the page
element creating the problem. Choose Print from the
File menu. You'll see a window displaying a progress
thermometer, which names each element as it down-
loads to the printer, starting with fonts. The last element before the next error message is your problem.

To get the file to print in a hurry, or if it won't
print at all, there are several options to try:

❖ Deselect all printer options in both dialog boxes
(such as Larger Print Area).

❖ Check Unlimited Downloadable Fonts or reduce
the number of fonts used.

❖ Print one page at a time. This will also show
which is the problem page; print the rest, then go
back and debug the problem.

❖ Try printing in low-resolution mode, which will
produce blocked-in graphics. If all you really need
is the text and positions of page elements, use the
"rough" option as the last resort, suppressing the
graphics. You can also suppress individual
graphics.

❖ Try selecting a different printer driver; the one
that came with your printer as well as more
generic ones.

Preprinted laser forms

If you are ordering or specifying printing on stationery or forms for use in a laser printer, make
sure that the ink to be used will be compatible—
that is, heat-resistant. For example, raised-ink
printing on laser stationery may fail to pass
through a laser printer, or leave a mess behind.

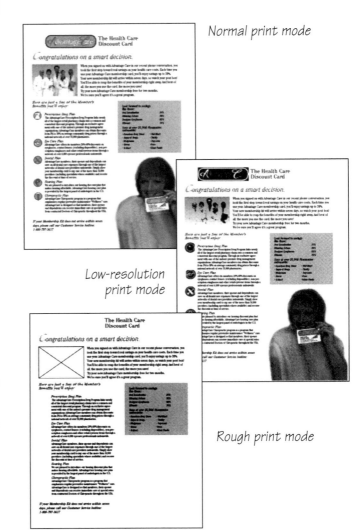

Normal print mode

Low-resolution
print mode

Rough print mode

Avoiding and fixing SCSI problems

To ensure trouble-free communication between SCSI devices (such as a SyQuest drive or scanner) and the CPU, be sure that all devices you plan to use are turned on at startup, or restart after turning on a device you have decided to use. This will help the system to recognize each link in the SCSI chain properly, and will give the appropriate drivers a chance to engage.

If you have trouble ejecting a volume in a SCSI disk, or cannot get a disk to eject, check to see if the File Sharing option is turned on. If so, turn it off and try again.

A SCSI chain can contain a maximum of seven devices, including extra internal drives, each with its own address and ID number. The CPU is always ID number 7. ID numbers bear no relation to the positions of devices on the chain. Never change any SCSI addresses, and be sure to turn off the entire system before plugging in or unplugging any devices on the SCSI chain.

Use only good quality, double-shielded cables (gold-plated connectors are best); you'll avoid many problems with signal noise. APS Technologies is one source for these. A three-foot cable is generally the most problem-free and versatile size. The total length of the SCSI chain, including connecting cables, should not exceed twenty feet.

Termination

Terminators are small devices or resistors that prevent noise and signal echoes in a SCSI chain, thereby guarding against data errors, sluggish performance, and crashes. The first and last devices on a SCSI chain should be terminated; normally, those in between should not. Most internal drives have factory-installed terminators. If more than three SCSI devices are on a chain, consider using an active terminator at the end of the chain.

A freeware utility called SCSI Probe is very useful for mounting stubborn SCSI device media (such as SyQuest cartridges or Zip disks). It can also give important information about devices on the SCSI chain, such as names and ID numbers.

Keep your SCSI device drivers updated with current software. SilverLining, another useful utility (which often comes bundled with SCSI drives), can aid in consolidating all devices on a chain with a single driver.

Monitors

When you shop for a monitor, considering its usage will give you an idea of the specs to watch for, including resolution.

Resolution depends on several factors:

❖ Number of pixels, measured horizontally and vertically

❖ Horizontal scan rate; the higher the rate, the better the image

❖ Refresh rate (the speed with which the screen redraws); the higher, the better: less screen flicker

A resolution of 1,280 x 1,024 or higher has become the standard for desktop publishing.

Another form of resolution to consider is color display. For image-editing and color work a display of 16.7 million colors at maximum resolution is desirable. To obtain this, you may need additional VRAM and a graphics board or card, especially with a larger display. Some monitors come bundled with these; others require a separate purchase. Graphics accelerators increase both the resolution and the speed of a monitor's display.

Look for a dot pitch rating of .28 mm or less.

Try to find a store where you can "test-drive" the monitor you are considering. Monitors vary widely, even those with the same model number. Bring some color test files with you on a floppy disk, to view on screen. Trade shows are great places to view and test the current crop of monitors.

Specify the system you will be using the monitor with, so you can get the appropriate adapters. Many monitors will work on either Mac or PC platforms with the correct hook-up.

Get the biggest and best monitor you can afford. A 20-inch monitor is the absolute minimum size for graphic work. Anti-glare coating is a useful feature.

A multisync monitor can offer some versatility: you can switch resolutions (and image sizes, correspondingly), depending on the task you want to perform.

Most monitors come with control software. When setting up, beware of conflicts between the monitor's software and any monitor controls resident in your system (for example, Photoshop's Kroll gamma control panel). Check with the manufacturer's tech support.

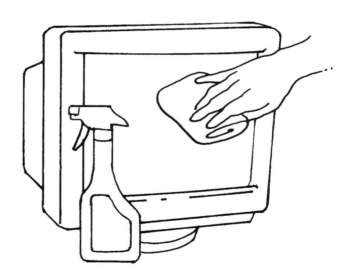

Monitor screens are dust magnets. You can clean yours with a soft cloth lightly sprayed with glass cleaner. Check the manufacturer's manual first to make sure the cleaner won't damage any special coatings on the screen.

System utilities

Utilities are small applications that add functionality to your system. INITs activate each time you start the computer, to perform specific functions (such as screen savers, font-management programs, and anti-virus applications), many of which can be customized. Control panels are accessed through the control panel menu, and can be set up to control various functions of hardware and system and individual software. Certain extensions (INITS), when residing together in a system folder, can conflict with each other, causing loss of functions and other problems, including system crashes. They also take up RAM. You may not want to have all of them active all the time.

For these reasons, it is helpful to install a program like Extension Manager (included with the Mac Operating System) or Conflict Catcher, which will enable you to identify at a glance all the utilities on your system, and to turn them off and on, globally or selectively, so you can isolate problem utilities.

Some types, uses, and examples of utilities

	Mac OS	PC/Windows
Compression	Stuffit Deluxe	PKZIP
Security	File Guard (ASD Software)	Norton Your Eyes Only
Virus protection	SAM (Symantec Antivirus)	Norton AntiVirus
Backup	Norton Utilities, Personal Backup (bundled with Zip drives), Copy Doubler	Cheyenne Backup
Memory control	operating system/control panel	operating system
Disk repair and data recovery	Disk First Aid, Norton Utilities	Norton Utilities
Font management	Suitcase, Master Juggler, Adobe Type Manager	operating system
Search tools	Norton Utilities	operating system
Multi-usage	Now Utilities	operating system

Designing for Electronic Delivery Systems
Building Web pages

The design of a World Wide Web page requires the same sensibility as design for print; however, many of the rules change. Web pages must be designed for ease of understanding by a wide audience. They must anticipate many different usage conditions. Although a truly comprehensive set of Web tips is beyond the scope of this book, here are some general guidelines for effective Web page design.

❖ *Apply the principles of good print design.*

Use consistent typograpy and graphics; don't mix text sizes and weights or illustration styles unnecessarily. Keep your audience in mind and use appropriate graphics, especially when providing cues for the viewer. Symbols that have meaning in the U.S.A. may be confusing to a viewer in Amsterdam or Hong Kong.

❖ *Let the viewer know what to expect.*

Build in visual or verbal clues as to what will appear on the following pages or screens.

When you use hypertext links, place them in logical locations on the page, such as at the beginning.

Label graphics with the ALT= feature, and include a warning for large graphics that will require a long wait while they download. When you provide a link to another Web page, notify the viewer if it is more than 100K in size.

❖ *Build in flexibility.*

The appearance of a Web page to a viewer depends upon the browser used by that viewer. Type styles and alignment, graphic appearance (or lack thereof), and page layout are at the mercy of the browser (and, occasionally, user-defined display options).

Netscape is currently the most popular browser. Use of the wider range of design options offered by Netscape, however, may produce a Web page that displays incoherent garbage to the roughly 30% of viewers who do not use Netscape, and therefore cannot access its more advanced features (such as two-column format, right justification, centering, and variable type size).

❖ *Limit page dimensions.*

On the average, Web pages will be viewed on 13- to 15-inch monitors with 800 x 600 pixel screen widths. Subtracting the screen area used by the browser, a page display area of 500 x 400 pixels remains. Graphic elements cannot be resized by the viewer, who is forced to scroll in order to view images larger than the viewing area (about two-thirds of the screen size). Restrict pictures and graphic elements to 400 pixels in width.

❖ *Keep pictures small.*

Size translates into time and storage space online. Large pictures take longer to download than smaller ones. A 28.8K-baud modem takes more than 60 seconds to display a 140K picture; several such images on a page increase the time accordingly. You will lose the viewer who has little reason to wait. Don't waste space on gratuitous pictures; use them only to convey important information.

❖ Use picture substitutes.

Potential viewers may have their browsers set to ignore graphics, in which case a verbal marker will be displayed instead of a picture. You can anticipate this by using the ALT= feature to display a one- to four-word description (such as "Widget product shot") of the graphic in its display area. This may be enough to convince the viewer to switch to graphic display mode.

Many browsers will not display text following a picture without knowing its size. Give the browser the dimensions of the picture with the width and height features of the image command, so that it can format the page's text while the picture is loading. This will allow the viewer to continue reading the text while waiting to see the image.

❖ Use GIF format for images.

Web browsers currently support only GIF or JPEG formats for images.

All browsers with graphics display capability will display GIF files. GIF images are limited to 256 colors, which is the number displayed on the average user's monitor. GIF file compression can significantly reduce file size without loss of image quality.

Two types of GIF files exist: interlaced (type 89a) and noninterlaced (type 87a). Save graphics and pictures as interlaced GIF files when possible. These images will be displayed as they load, rather than requiring the viewer to wait for the entire image to load before it is displayed.

JPEG format should be used only when 24-bit color is absolutely necessary. A high ratio of JPEG compression can produce significant loss of quality; ratios from 10:1 to 30:1 are acceptable. About 20% of Web browsers will not support JPEG, displaying text markers instead.

❖ Limit page file size.

A viewer surfing the Web is unlikely to wait for long while a page loads; size is critical.

Keep graphic elements such as buttons and dingbats to 2K or less. Limit larger images to 25K or less, and limit their number on the page.

A Web page without a picture will hold only a short paragraph or two of text. One typeset, printed page will equal two to four screen pages. Limit the scrolling required to four or five screens; warn the viewer if there will be more than this.

Remember that Web browsers will mangle or simply ignore information they don't understand. Keep yours simple, and go for the lowest common denominator.

❖ Keep text concise and informative.

Underlined blue text is standard for hypertext links, changing to magenta after a visit to the site.

Web image files

Line art scanned as line for print use

Line art scanned as grayscale for Web use

Line art scanned for use in print is generally scanned as line art. Scanned line art destined for Web page use will retain more of its original image integrity if scanned and saved as a grayscale image.

Keep GIF files smaller than 20 KB if possible, by using smaller dimensions, fewer colors, and judicious dithering. Most photos look okay in 32 colors (5-bit adaptive); some art can look acceptable in 8 or 16 colors. The following shows the results of scaling down a file's color depth:

RGB file (320 x 240 pixels)	243 KB
saved as	
GIF file (8-bit adaptive indexed color)	72 KB
GIF file (5-bit adaptive indexed color)	44 KB
GIF file (4-bit adaptive indexed color)	32 KB
GIF file (3-bit adaptive indexed color)	23 KB

Help your audience to navigate more easily

To facilitate online searches, embed key words related to your Web page subject on your page and spec the text colors to match the background. The words will be invisible on screen, but a browser will find them if any of the words are used in a search.

When referencing linked spots, adopt a consistent style, such as text with a special color or a box under it, to designate linked information.

Since people often like to print out online pages, keep your text against a light background, or tack on a black-and-white text-only section.

Web text

```
<img src="bskt.gif">

Has catnip left your cat bored?  Kookie Kitty Kurl-Q's will keep your
kitty or cat constantly moving.  Three Kurl-Q's per package.  Your
cat can chase, swoosh or pounce all day.  An exciting and safe kitty toy
to add to your collection

<p>

Kookie Kitty Kurl-Q's

<hr>

$4.50    Quantity_____

<hr>
```

Add extra return spaces in your HTML text file, as shown above. This allows easier editing and structuring, and the spaces won't be displayed by web browsers like Netscape.

Has catnip left your cat bored? Kookie Kitty Kurl-Q's will keep your kitty or cat constantly moving. Three Kurl-Q's per package. Your cat can chase, swoosh or pounce all day. An exciting and safe kitty toy to add to your collection
Kookie Kitty Kurl-Q's
$4.50   Quantiy____   ☒

● **Order**
● **Home Page**

Glossary

aliasing. The unpleasant stepped or jagged edges of unfiltered bitmapped images. Most image-editing applications have anti-aliasing features.

application. Software program designed for a specific task (such as the image-editing application Photoshop).

APR. See automatic image replacement.

archive. Long-term online or offline storage. In digital systems, files are generally archived (i.e., saved) onto some form of hard disc, magnetic tape, floppy disc, or cartridge.

ASCII (American Standard Code for Information Interchange). The byte coding for the standard character set used by most computers. ASCII files are written in the code without any formatting commands and are used to move text files between computers and applications.

automatic image replacement. The process by which high-resolution image files are substituted ("swapped") for low-resolution place-holders (FPOs) when the document is output. Also called automatic picture replacement (APR) or Open Press Interface (OPI).

background processing. Processing work performed by the computer to carry out the instructions of the operator while other activities are being performed, frequently done without any evidence on the monitor screen.

baseline. The (imaginary) line upon which type rests.

Bézier curve. A curve, named after Pierre Bézier, that is defined by four control points which are at the ends of the two direction lines tangent to each curve. Curves produced in drawing programs are Bézier curves.

binary. A coding or counting system with only two symbols or conditions, like on/off or zero/one; the format for storing data in computers. The term "digital" has a similar meaning.

bit. A shortened form of the term "binary digit," the smallest unit of information that can be stored in a computer.

bitmap. A pixel-by-pixel description of an image. Each pixel is a separate element, composing a matrix to make up the whole bitmapped image. Also referred to as a raster image. TIFF, PICT, GIF, and some EPS files are bitmapped.

blend. The even distribution of shapes, tints, or colors or both between two objects. Also called a gradient fill, vignette, or fountain when filling a defined area.

BPS (Bits Per Second). Measure of how fast data can be transferred.

byte. Unit of memory in a computer, consisting of eight bits. One byte expresses image intensity at one point (pixel) of an image in one channel. Or it can represent one letter, number, or symbol in the ASCII code.

calibration. Fine tuning of monitor, imagesetter, proofing, and printing devices to produce desired results on press.

CD-ROM (Compact Disc, Read Only Memory). CDs can contain a mixture of photos, motion pictures, sound, and text or other programs. Each disc can hold up to 650 megabytes.

CEP (Color Electronic Prepress). High-end prepress workstations.

choke trap. The intentional overlap of a lighter background onto a darker object to compensate for misregistration on press.

click. To press and immediately release the mouse button.

clipping path. A vector path, drawn around a bitmap image and embedded in its file, which defines the image's edges when it is imported to a page layout program.

clone. An exact duplicate of certain image data.

CMYK (Cyan Magenta Yellow Black). The four process printing ink colors, combined on press to approximate the full visible spectrum. K is the abbreviation for black.

coated stock. Paper that has a light clay or plastic coating, which can have either a matte or glossy surface.

color call outs. Names used to define colors in electronic art; specified in the color palette from the menu bar. Various color models can be set up, including CMYK and spot colors. The color selected will appear in the list of colors and can be applied like a type style.

comp. Comprehensive artwork or dummy used to represent the general color and arrangement of a layout.

compound path. A group of two or more paths, with at least one reversed path, which can create the effect of transparent areas, or "holes" in the artwork.

control point. The point that determines where a line segment starts or ends. Invisible unless any segment of the path is selected. Control points that end Bézier curve segments have direction controls associated with them. Also called anchor point.

crop marks. Marks that show where a page is to be trimmed, or which sections of a photo or transparency should be reproduced.

CPU (Central Processing Unit). A large chip inside the console, the "brains" of the computer, where data processing takes place.

cursor. The "pointer" on a computer display screen, visible in various forms, such as ">", an arrow, or an I-beam (called an insertion point). The cursor is controlled by a mouse, keyboard, or other hand-manipulated input device.

custom color. Color created using proprietary, premixed printing inks, such as PMS colors or special ink mixes. Also referred to as spot colors.

DCS (Desktop Color Separation). A format that creates five PostScript files for each color image.

default settings. Information entered into software programs that remains the same each time the application is launched, unless modified by the user.

digitizing tablet. Input device consisting of a drawing surface connected to the computer and a pressure-sensitive wand. When combined with appropriate software, this combination can emulate such traditional media as pen, brush, pencil, or charcoal.

direct-to-film. Term meaning that the output from the computer file onto film can be used to produce the final plates for printing without further adjustment.

disk. A flat, circular plate, coated with a magnetic material, on which data may be stored by selective magnetization of portions of the surface. May be a flexible, "floppy" disk or rigid "hard" disk.

display. Any typeface designed to be used at large sizes, as when used for signs, headlines, or graphics rather than for text body copy. Also, a computer's monitor.

document. An electronic file, which may contain text, art, page layout, or other elements.

dot. An often-confusing term with various interpretations.
A halftone dot and a pixel are not related. Pixels are the basic elements of bitmapped images and monitor displays, and are also units of resolution (pixels per inch). They have fixed size, but variable density. Halftone dots form the matrix into which the tones of a photo are broken to make them printable. They have fixed density but variable size.
Halftone resolution is expressed in lines per inch (lpi). In an input scanner or continuous-tone output device (e.g., dye-sublimation printer), resolution is measured in pixels per inch (ppi).
Scanner resolution is sometimes quoted in dpi (dots per inch) but this can be misleading, because here the word "dot" really means "pixel." When referring to a continuous-tone scanner, "dpi" should be replaced by "ppi" (points per inch or pixels per inch) or "lpi" (lines per inch) to avoid confusion.

dot gain. The amount by which a halftone dot grows from film to plate to press.

dpi (dots per inch or dots per millimeter). Measurement of the resolution of a printer or imagesetter. More than 1,000 dpi is considered to be type-set quality. Desktop laser printers range from 300 to 600 dpi.

drag. To hold down the mouse button while moving the cursor.

draw program. A vector-based application, such as Illustrator or Freehand.

drum scanner. A high-end input device, in which the art is taped to the surface of a spinning drum. A narrow beam of light passes through the drum and produces digital electrical signals resulting in a high-resolution image.

emulsion. The photosensitive layer on a piece of film or paper.

EPS(Encapsulated PostScript). Format of a document written in the PostScript language, containing all of the code necessary to print the file or export it to another application.

file. The digital database that electronically represents either a picture image or a line image, or a set of instructions (program) for the CPU. Once a digital file has been created, it can be saved in a variety of formats.

film. Material output by an imagesetter, used to make printing plates. One piece of film and one plate are required for each color.

film recorder. Device for converting digital data into film output. Continuous-tone recorders produce color photographs, either as transparencies, prints, or negatives. Halftone recorders produce film with halftone dots that can be used to make printing plates.

flatbed scanner. A scanner in which the material to be scanned is placed flat, rather than wrapped around a drum. Most desktop scanners are flatbeds.

flip. To rotate an image, such as a photo, 180 degrees horizontally, from top to bottom.

flop. To rotate an image, such as a photo, 180 degrees on a vertical axis, from left to right.

font. A complete set of type characters in a single size, style, and weight, such as 12-point Helvetica Regular. Often used interchangeably with "typeface."

FPO (For Position Only). A low-resolution image used to indicate placement on a layout, to be replaced by a high-resolution image for reproduction.

gamma control. The relationship between the tone values in an image file and the tone values produced by an output device. When adjusted as part of calibration, it affects only the screen appearance of an image and not the image itself.

GCR (Gray Component Replacement). The substitution of black ink for relative values of cyan, magenta, and yellow.

gigabyte. Unit of computer memory consisting of about one thousand million bytes (a thousand megabytes). Actual value is 1,073,741,824 bytes.

global. A change that affects an entire document, as opposed to "local" changes.

gradient fill. A gradated blend between colors or tints.

grayscale. Gradation of tones between black and white on a computer monitor, or in a contiuous-tone image.

greeking. A representation of text using Latin or random words, or horizontal lines, for comp purposes.

group. To combine two or more objects so they function as a single object.

halftone. Conversion of a continuous-tone photographic image into a pattern of various dot sizes for single-color reproduction. Usually used in reference to black-and-white printing; a process-color halftone is called a separation.

high-end system. A prepress system consisting of computer processors, high-resolution scanner, and imagesetting equipment, in contrast to low-end systems typified by the "desktop publishing" setup of personal computer, low-resolution scanner, and laser printer.

image-editing program. An application designed to manipulate bitmapped images (such as scans of photos). Examples: Photoshop and Painter.

imagesetter. The prepress machine that produces the film or photographic paper output from which printers' plates are made; basically an extremely high-quality printer.

imposed flats. Pages prepared for film or press, arranged in "forms," as they will be printed on a sheet, then folded and trimmed.

input. Any and all information that a computer receives from an external source, whether from keystrokes, a scanner, disk or tape, or a file received via modem.

interface. The system (hardware and software) that ties two components of a system together, so they can communicate or transfer data.

K. (1) A kilobyte; 1,024 bytes. (2) Abbreviation for black in CMYK color printing

knockout. An area that "shows through" an image. In an image with white type on a black background, the white type "knocks out" of the background. Also called a reverse.

LAB. An abbreviation of CIE L*a*b, a color model developed by the Commission Internationale d'Eclairage as an international standard for color measurement. Lab color is designed to be device-independent. It consists of three components: luminance (lightness), a (green to red chroma), and b (blue to yellow).

layer. A designated level in artwork that allows a portion of the artwork to be easily selected and edited.

leading. The amount of vertical space between lines of type.

letterspacing. The space between individual letters. Increase or decrease letterspacing to increase legibility or to achieve a certain design effect. There are two ways to control letterspacing: tracking affects the space between all letters equally, and kerning affects space between individual letters.

line frequency. Number of halftone dots per linear inch in a halftone screen. The finer the screen, the more detail can be portrayed in the final printed piece. Also called line screen resolution.

marquee. An outline drawn with a selection tool to select objects in an image or page.

mask. A temporary stencil restricting the action of various functions to a selected area within the picture. Masks can be drawn manually (with a stylus or mouse) or created automatically keyed to specific density levels or hue values in the picture, similar to photolith masking in an enlarger.

MB (Megabyte). One million bytes (actually 1,048,576 bytes) or 1,000 K.

Mhz (MegaHertz). One million cycles per second. A measure of how many operations or cycles a computer's CPU can complete in one second.

moiré. The distracting and unattractive optical pattern that occurs when two or more screen tints are overlaid incorrectly.

mouse. A small, handheld pointing device that, when moved on flat surface, causes a corresponding movement of a cursor on the monitor.

NTSC (National Television Standards Committee). A color standard for television and other video with 32,000 possible colors. Based on the RGB color model.

OCR (Optical Character Recognition). Programs that can read printed characters by scanning into a computer.

offset printing. Method that uses that uses an intermediate roller to transfer a printed image from plate to paper. Also called offset lithography.

outline. A vector-based description of a font or image's shape. PostScript fonts contain outlines; PostScript graphics (such as Illustrator EPS files) include outlines. Since outlines are mathematical descriptions, they are infinitely scalable. Also called path.

output. A product of the computer as a result of its processing. Examples: A page of RC paper; negative film.

overprint. To print a color over another color. The overprinting color may cover or mix with the overprinted color. Δ1Black type is commonly overprinted on other colors.

path. See outline.

PMS (Pantone Matching System). A color defining and matching system commonly used in the printing industry.

PDL (Page Description Language). Formatting language for fonts, color, and graphics. PostScript is the most popular.

photo CD. A method of storing photographic images on a CD-ROM.

pica. Typographer's measurement unit. There are 12 points to a pica, 12 picas to an inch.

pixel (picture element). A single dot on a computer display; the smallest visual unit in a bitmap file.

platform. The combination of proprietary operating system and hardware. Common platforms are PC (Microsoft/IBM) and Macintosh.

plug-in. A module supplied separately from a program for creating special effects or functions.

points. Typographer's measurement system. There are 72 points to the inch. See also pica.

PostScript. A programming language that gives output devices precise instructions for printing out encoded files. Also referred to as a page description language. Developed by Adobe, PostScript Level 1 was later joined by PostScript Level 2, which offers additional controls.

PPD (PostScript Printer Description). The document used to set the default information for the specific printer or imagesetter in use, including its dot resolution, available page sizes, color support, and acceptable screen rulings and angles.

ppi (pixels per inch). Measures of the amount of scanned information. The higher the ppi, the finer the image.

prepress. Document preparation leading to the actual printing of reproductions on press; includes scanning, color separation, image manipulation, film output, and stripping.

process colors. The four printing inks, cyan (C), magenta (M), yellow (Y), and black (K—to avoid confusion with blue), used to create the full spectrum of color on a printed page.

processing. The "number crunching" computer function by which instructions from the user are carried out. Processing usually involves a noticeable amount of time.

RAM (Random Access Memory). The part of a computer's memory that may be used for temporary storage of information; the computer's "work area." A greater amount of RAM usually offers faster image manipulation or faster background processing in high resolution retouching systems.

raster image. A pixel-based (bitmapped) image information file, in which the image is expressed by a very fine grid. Each grid cell, or pixel, is stored as a set of numbers for CMYK, RGB, or intensity, hue, and saturation values. Content of image, tint, and hue are recorded pixel by pixel in order of location.

RC paper. Resin-coated paper, a glossy medium on which an imagesetter outputs high-resolution text and image files, usually as a black-and-white positive.

registration. The process of lining up colors on press in the printing process.

registration marks. Marks used to align the various pieces of film during the stripping process.

removable media. Types of hard disk enclosed in a cartridge that can be changed in the drive.

resolution. A measure of the amount of detail or sharpness visible in an image or attainable in an imaging system.

RGB (Red Green Blue). (1) The additive primary colors that make up the display on a computer monitor. (2) A color system used for various electronic delivery systems, such as digital video and online graphics.

RIP (Raster Image Processor). A high-end device used to convert the output of a prepress computer system into a format (dots, or rasters) usable by an imagesetter.

RISC (Reduced Instruction Set Computing). A fast processor that utilizes a relatively small set if instructions. Power PC computer chips are based on RISC technology.

ROM (Read-Only Memory). Computer memory that may be read by the CPU, but cannot be altered.

rosette. The circular dot pattern that occurs when screen tints or process colors are overlaid correctly.

scanning. The conversion of an analog original (art or photo) to a digital file.

screen tint. A screened percentage of a solid color, measured in lines per inch. The greater the screen tint, the larger the halftone dot and the more intense the color.

separation. The process of breaking down an image into component ink colors (such as CMYK for process printing). The resulting electronic file or set of film is abbreviated "sep."

silhouette. An image outlined or with background eliminated in a photograph or piece of art.

spot color. A custom ink color as opposed to a process ink.

spread. A two-page arrangement, either reader spreads (two facing pages of a publication) or printer spreads (two pages in their printing imposition order).

spread trap. The intentional overlap of a lighter object into a darker background to compensate for misregistration problems on press.

stochastic. A halftone process utilizing dots of varying frequency and uniform size.

stroke. The line defining the edge of an image, or a line.

style. A design variation of a typeface, such as regular, italic, bold, or bold italic.

system. An integrated assembly of hardware and software designed to work together to implement a given set of applications.

SWOP (Specifications for Web Offset Publications). A standard for printing production.

template. An image that may be traced or duplicated to create identical new artwork. Also, a document saved for use as a model for similar ones.

TIFF (Tagged Image File Format). A file format for exchanging bitmapped images between applications.

tiled page. A page output in sections, when the file's page size is larger than the output device's capacity.

trap. The overlap needed to ensure that a slight misalignment or movement of the separations on press will not cause unacceptable misregistration in the printed piece.

UCR (Under Color Removal). A CMYK printing film preparation setting that uses the black plate to add depth to shadows and neutral colors.

unsharp masking. A procedure for increasing the apparent detail of an image, performed either by the input scanner or by image processing.

vector image. An image system that uses basic geometric shapes, such as Bézier curves, to create a graphic image. Rescaling can be performed with greater accuracy than with bitmap data. Also called object oriented. Draw programs produce and edit vector images.

write. The function of copying a file from disk to tape. Also, sometimes used to describe the transfer of information from the internal computer memory to a disk.

WYSIWYG (What You See Is What You Get). Term referring to the image on the screen being exactly what you get when output is printed.

YCC (Kodak Photo CD). Format developed by Kodak for storing images in multiple resolutions. To print this type of scanned image, it must first be converted to RGB and then CMYK.

Sources

An exhaustive list of equipment and software suppliers would require an entire book. The selection given here includes a wide range of products and manufacturers. Many of these companies make other products not mentioned here; I have only included those that the companies are best known for.

These are for the most part low-end products, meaning that they are suitable for use on desktop equipment, as opposed to high-end use. Inclusion here does not constitute an endorsement, nor would each one fit everyone's particular needs. Shop judiciously and ask lots of questions.

Adobe   800 833-6687
http://www.adobe.com
(software: Photoshop, Streamline, Illustrator, Pagemill, Type Reunion, Type Manager (ATM), fonts, etc.)

Agfa 800 424-8973
http://www.agfahome.com
(scanners)

Aladdin Systems   800 732-8881
(Stuffit and other utilities)

Alsoft   800 257-6381
(Master Juggler)

Apple   800 776-2333
http://www.apple.com
(computers, printers, scanners, software)

APS Technologies
800 374-5681
(catalog of computer systems, drives, supplies, and accessories)

Azalea Software, Inc. 800 48-ASOFT
info@azalea.com
http://www.azalea.com
(bar code software)

Casady & Greene   800 359-4920
(Conflict Catcher)

CDW (Computer Discount Warehouse)
800 500-4239
(hardware & software catalog)

Corel   800 772-6735
(Corel Draw, Corel PhotoPaint, etc.)

Dantz Development 510 253-3000
(Retrospect)

The Designsoft Company
630 858-5363
(Designsoft, Prowheel, other software)

Drawing tablets, from Kurta, Calcomp and Wacom, to mention just a few, are available from many computer stores and catalogs, including those listed here.

Dubl-Click Software   800 266-9525
(MenuFonts)

Epson   800 922-8911
http://www.epson.com
(scanners; printers—inkjet [Stylus Pro])

Fargo   800 327-4522
(printers—dye sublimation)

Focus Enhancements   800-538-8866
(Redux)

Fractal Design   800 297-COOL
(software: Painter, Dabbler, etc.)

GCC   800 422-7777
(printers—grayscale laser [optimized for grayscale work])

Global Village Communication
800 736-4821
(fax modems and software)

Hewlett-Packard   800 752-0900
http://www.hp.com
(scanners; printers—laser and inkjet)

Inset   203 740-2400
(Hijaak Browser)

Iomega   800 my-stuf
(Zip drive removable media)

Mainstay   805 484-9400
(Captivate)

Metatools (formerly HSC software)
805 566-6385
http://www.metatools.com
(software: applications and plug-ins)

Now Software   800 237-2078
(Now Utilities)

PKWare
(PKZIP; shareware, available online)

The PC Zone 800 258-2088
(hardware and software catalog: Norton Utilities, Cheyenne Backup and AntiVirus)

Quark   800 788-7835
(Quark XPress)

SCSI Probe: freeware, available online or bundled with removable disk software

Symantec   800 441-7234
(SAM, Norton Utilities, DiskDoubler, AutoDoubler, Suitcase)

Synex   718 499-6923
(Bar Code Pro for Mac and Windows)

Therapeutic Appliance Group
800 457-5535
(Handeeze Musician's Glove)

UMAX   800 562-0311
(scanners)

Visioneer 415 812-6400
(PaperPort scanners)

Xante   800 926-8839
(laser printers)

Index